TURNING
Daily Struggle
INTO
Opportunities

TURNING
Daily Struggle
INTO
Opportunities

MARTIN VAN HELDEN

Rev. date: 01/11/2023

To order additional copies of this book, contact:
Xlibris
AU TFN: 1 800 844 927 (Toll Free inside Australia)
AU Local: (02) 8310 8187 (+61 2 8310 8187 from outside Australia)
www.Xlibris.com.au
Orders@Xlibris.com.au
849797

CONTENTS

INTRODUCTION

Difficulties abound in real life. Some individuals seem to be able to confidently take on any obstacle, while others consistently falter. Facing adversity head-on is extremely rewarding for pittas because of the feeling of success it offers. You seem to actively seek difficulty. Experience is life's most powerful instrument for progress, and your higher self wants you to learn and expand your horizons.

The difficulty is that it's easy to become stuck in a rut and stop seeing the potential lesson in the repeated setbacks you experience. When difficulties escalate into issues, they may quickly lead to feelings of hopelessness and anger.

You can get through this because you're an active participant in making your world what it is. If you have a healthy dose of self-awareness and accountability, you may start ascending the ladder of enlightenment, where difficulties are transformed from obstacles into chances to see your best self.

Here are some strategies you will find in this book that will help you overcome your own unique difficulties.

Engage the Obstacle

This is generally the first and most crucial step, yet it is often the one that gets overlooked the most. Rather than tackling the problem head-on, many people waste their time trying to find a workaround or become despondent at how difficult the situation is. A mountain of clothes or unfinished tasks is overlooked, along with more pressing concerns. Putting off a task won't make it disappear. Both large and little obstacles may be approached in the same way. Simply looking at what's in front of you is the most useful thing you can do.

Pay Attention

Remember the importance of your presence. If you make it a habit to face adversity head-on, even when you fail, you'll soon realise that most of the things you thought were difficult weren't. We should see life's difficulties as signs from the cosmos. Silent awareness may be cultivated via meditation, making it a useful technique for refocusing attention inward during trying times.

You may learn more about the issue and how it impacts you by asking yourself the right kinds of questions.

What makes this a difficult task?

To what extent do I think I can tackle this test and come out on top?

Is there a way to predict the results of my efforts?

When asked, "What happens if I don't succeed?"

These questions aren't designed to provide answers but rather to assist you to get a more holistic understanding of the difficulty at hand and your own response to it.

You need to look inside yourself for an answer.

The insights of others may be invaluable in guiding you towards your own realisation, but no one can ever really "fix" your issues for you. No matter who is in the position of power or cooperation with you, ultimately it is up to you to determine how you will handle the issue. Finding answers elsewhere will only delay facing your own shortcomings. Think about what you can do, what you have access to, and what your options are. It's possible that you'll need to solicit the aid of others, but ultimately the burden will fall on your shoulders. The sooner you accept the challenge, the sooner it ceases to be a problem.

Recognise Yourself

Problems might be seen as developmental challenges. This expansion results from potentiality, your potential, which is both boundless and always at work in every minute of your existence. Accept it about yourself. You are infinite possibility going through the illusion of confinement. All you need to break through that fictitious wall of limitations is a few well-placed challenges. It's up to you to determine whether you're bounded by your own awareness and love or if you're an expanding development in both. Pick the second and give that so-called difficulty another look.

It's not random that certain obstacles feel insurmountable while others seem to provide no difficulty at all. This is not because they are inherently superior to you. The key is in one's state of mind. Those who must deal with difficult jobs have learned to see them in a different light.

Let Go of the Result

Worrying too much about future results is usually what makes a little problem seem insurmountable. The most daunting aspects of the trial begin to fade away as you begin to concentrate on the process rather than the outcome. If you focus on finishing the job at hand rather than dwelling on the possible outcomes, you will gain control of the situation.

Even the most daunting obstacles may be overcome with confidence and poise if you keep your mind and body steady.

CHAPTER ——————— 1

Embrace It

There will be many challenges to overcome throughout your lifetime. When hardships arise, do you accept them as opportunities for growth, or do you want to hide under a rock? Nothing can be done to avoid trouble; life is full of them.

It might be challenging to remember that difficulties cropping up regularly are par for your course. Although some experiences are more powerful than others, they all impact who we are deep down.

To accept difficulties as opportunities, what does it mean to do so?

As humans, we often wish we could avoid dealing with vexing problems in life. To embrace a challenge is to meet a strange and difficult situation with the will to succeed rather than give up and give in.

In these situations, you must have an open mind. Don't see them as insurmountable obstacles; seek refuge from addressing them. On the other hand, you welcome and embrace these challenges, and you rise to meet them head-on. Doing so contributes to your development and gives your life more significance.

How Do You Accept Life's Challenges?

It would help if you didn't allow the hardships you're experiencing to destroy you. The key is to examine your mindset and your reaction to such challenges when they arise.

Take hold of these methods to push through difficulties and emerge victorious.

Choose to Accept the Challenge

When a difficulty presents itself, choose to accept it. Keeping a good disposition is essential.

Because how you respond to challenges is crucial. Keeping a positive outlook will go a long way towards alleviating the anxiety brought on by the circumstance.

The more difficult situations become, the more worried you get. As a result, it's easy to have feelings of helplessness and bafflement. Maybe you've been feeling like a victim lately. However, the reality is that life is beyond your control.

When you need to learn more to make an informed decision, avoid panicking or giving up. This is an excellent chance to rise to the challenge.

You have control over whether or not you let yourself get overwhelmed. Instead of giving up on adversity, take stock and use the experience to forge new strengths.

In the face of difficulty, you should square your shoulders and rush in headfirst.

There is no room for giving up at this point. But resolve to succeed despite the odds. You've just taken the first step in defeating your formidable foes.

Be willing to be uncomfortable and accept it.

As painful as they may be in the moment, many of life's events ultimately serve a higher purpose.

Even if your issue seems impossible and your motivation is low, acknowledging, accepting, and even welcoming it is essential. It may be pretty upsetting and painful to experience.

All kinds of things may cause people to face anxieties, from money problems to loss to natural calamities. This discomfort may make you think your world is collapsing around you. Once you get beyond that rough patch though, you'll feel much better and stronger overall.

Please don't run away from these difficulties. It's essential to keep in mind that bad times do not persist forever. It's possible to engage them head-on and emerge victorious.

Treat It Carefully and Slowly

Dealing with difficult circumstances may cause a wide range of feelings. You might be filled with optimism one minute and utterly befuddled the next. Because of this, you may feel drained of energy.

It's essential to take things slowly. Just take things as they are. Try not to dwell on the difficulties at hand. Instead, take a few deep breaths to help you relax and get your bearings.

At this stage, it's tempting to let your thoughts wander to the worst-case scenario.

There's no better time than now to do whatever you need to counter this, whether it's praying, meditating, or repeating positive affirmations or mantras. Now is when it's most important to take care of your mental health.

Whether you need to say it aloud or mentally repeat it, it makes no difference. Calm down, feel better, and find hope, comfort, and serenity with this.

The further vital problem is that we often neglect to care for ourselves when challenging situations. Nonetheless, it would help if you treated yourself with kindness. Please take care of yourself. Nutrient-rich diets and regular exercise are essential for maintaining good health.

Your Backup Team

If you're going through a rough patch and experiencing a wide range of emotions, know that you're not alone.

What a difference it can make to have encouraging friends and family members close by. They will help you keep your chin up when things become rough. They will inspire you and help you feel better.

These people behind you will give you the strength to overcome the difficulty.

You will support one another through the good times and the bad. You and your band of allies will meet the challenges head-on. You will cheer each other on and enjoy your successes.

Accept and Appreciate Your Challenges

The idea that you should be thankful for your difficulties may not make sense initially. But give it some thought. Accepting difficulties as opportunities for growth and strengthening the mind is the path to success.

This is why you'll emerge from the experience more robust and formidable than ever. There is no greater sense of accomplishment than triumph over adversity.

Use a Joke

You may not believe it's a good idea to find the funny side of things at a difficult time. However, studies have proven that humour plays a vital role in our everyday lives.

Comedy can help you relax and deal with difficult situations. Connecting with others is beneficial as well.

We may not be able to change things, but we can make them funnier. This helps to calm your anxieties. Get together with loved ones or visit a comedy club to laugh it up. Laughter is a potent medicine that can help heal wounds and bring people together.

Why Is It Good to Take on Adventures?

If you're having difficulty seeing the positive in a challenging circumstance, switch your frame of mind. Persevering through adversity is a terrific way to learn valuable lessons.

A wide range of positive outcomes is associated with taking up challenging tasks. Here are some of them:

- Facilitates the development of an attitude of appreciation
- Improves one's mental fortitude
- When you work hard, you eventually learn to value your successes.
- You feel more specific in your talents.
- It helps you become more equipped to deal with challenges.
- Individuality will begin to shine through.
- Aids in showcasing originality and resourcefulness
- Helpful in developing feelings of sympathy and understanding for others

Struggles often occur in human existence. You may learn a great deal about life from encounters like this. It's crucial to remember that adversity may be a catalyst for personal development.

Without obstacles, it would be impossible to learn new things, develop as a person, become more resilient, and ultimately become your best self.

Reasons Why You Shouldn't Run Away from Your Problems

Escaping from a difficult situation simply further isolates you from a workable resolution. Solving the issue is the simplest way out of it.

We all have those times when we feel like the world is conspiring against us and nothing we do will ever be enough to overcome the obstacles we face, whether socially, professionally, financially, physically, or in any other facet of life.

When things become rough, we usually do the logical thing and either put things off or try to avoid them.

Think back on the last time you tried to rebuild a broken relationship, whether it be with a friend, family member, or co-worker or even with yourself in terms of your fitness and health.

We prefer to ignore problems in the hopes that they will go away if we don't give them any thought, or we blame external factors or other people when our efforts yield no results.

This provides temporary solace since the onus of responsibility has been transferred to an external source. Why does escaping the issue(s) at hand seem to be the path of least resistance?

There are several short-term benefits to evading a problem: the monster can't see you anymore, you've avoided harm, the spotlight is now on something or someone else, you feel hopeful that things will improve, and so on.

Know first that "running away from your troubles is a race you will never win." The reason is that you will eventually have to face them and take care of them regardless of how long it has been or how far away it is.

Instead of trying to avoid, manipulate, or stifle fears, it's important to learn about them by observing and studying them in their natural habitats. We are to learn about fear, not how to escape from it.

In addition, you can never lose yourself since you are constantly following closely behind.

The second piece of advice is to never place blame on anybody. The finest individuals leave you with memories, the worst with a lesson, and the most pleasant among them leave you with just enjoyment.

If you try to avoid your issues by running away from them, you may wind up having to confront them again, at which point they will be twice as difficult to handle. In addition, by the time you're done running, you'll be thousands of miles away from the people who care about you, and the issue will still be there, but now no one can assist you.

Last but not least, we can't solve the issues using the same thinking that we used when we created them. It's not easy to keep going when times are rough. The act of fleeing from a difficult situation is typically the easiest solution.

However, avoiding responsibility will never solve the problem. When you realise there's no escaping your issues, you've got to learn to face them head-on or die trying. And if that's the case, why not right now from your vantage point?

When we remain and keep going, even when the going gets tough, that's when we win. Stay in the game and never give up! Instead of seeking outside for solutions to your troubles and worries, you should go inside yourself and figure out how you can fight them.

First, stop what you're doing, take a breath, think about what you're thinking, and then do something about it. Only by looking back can you see how things fit together. The act of introspection is humbling since it might reveal aspects of one's character that one was previously unaware even existed. Think back on the options you were given and the ones you ultimately choose.

Don't put the blame on other people or external events since it will prevent you from figuring out the root of your difficulties. And if you do it again, you may finally come to terms with the fact that you have only yourself to blame. Put an end to assigning blame and begin seeking solutions.

Third, avoid wallowing in self-pity. We're all susceptible to its seductive pull since feeling sorry for oneself is so natural. It provides temporary relief by isolating the person from the source of his or her suffering. Admit your flaws and your successes, accept your talents and weaknesses, and actively seek ways to improve.

Observe a trend or pattern to learn more about the situation; just as triumphs leave traces, so do setbacks. You need to just keep your thoughts and emotions engaged to see the pattern. If you could figure out what they are, you'd know how to get out of there. Rather than being roadblocks, difficulties should be seen as signposts pointing the way to improvement; as such, you should devote effort to figuring out how to overcome them.

Avoid letting your issues drive you. Instead, let your hopes and aspirations serve as your motivation in times of difficulty.

Practice Self-Compassion

When did you last yell at yourself? Have you ever criticised yourself for a wrong action?

Perhaps you've been quite critical of someone, only to be much more critical of yourself afterward.

Being hard on oneself is common, and we do it more often than we give ourselves credit. But suppose there was a more suitable approach. Self-compassion is forgiving and accepting oneself despite imperfections and treating oneself kindly. It's more challenging than it seems, but we may form a lasting routine with practice.

Some of these methods may be helpful if you pass harsh judgment or self-criticism without good cause. Some may not interest you, but you never know which ones may strike a chord and be helpful.

Positive connotations are attached to persons who exemplify compassion, and those who are compassionate are often seen as sympathetic, kind, and understanding.

To whom would you attribute these characteristics? Perhaps it's a well-known person who was instrumental in relieving the pain of others, such as Princess Diana or Mother Teresa. Or maybe it is your mother or closest friend who is always there for you and provides unwavering support.

These kind individuals are well-known and well admired by others, and they often rank among our circle's happiest members. A room filled with them is instantly brightened and the mood of the people in it lifted. In addition to being an exemplary example of compassion, they also set off chain reactions and motivate others to follow suit. It's possible you're a kind person who actively seeks to ease the suffering of others.

Many of us, particularly those who see ourselves as empaths, are ready to help individuals in our close circle of friends, family, and loved ones when we see their challenges and are moved to do so. While we are quick to assist those in need, there is often one individual who is denied the benefit of our kindness because we are too busy helping someone else.

Instead, we show ourselves nothing but disdain, suffering, and condemnation. We place excessive emphasis on the quality of our work, are harshly critical of our efforts, and have high standards for ourselves. Just picture yourself addressing other people the way you talk to yourself. Someone who commits a mistake is comforted by the reassurance that "everyone makes errors." When we screw up though, we tend to scold ourselves and say things like "You're so foolish!"

The standard response to a buddy who expresses dissatisfaction with their physical appearance is "You're so lovely!" However, many of us feel disgust and guilt when we examine our reflections. Instead, try imagining how it would feel to talk to yourself in the same manner you talk to other people.

Many academics and mental health professionals have taken an interest in self-compassion studies as a natural extension of mindfulness. It inspires us to be nicer and more loving in the connection we have with ourselves every day.

Self-compassion, as defined by noted researcher and therapist Dr Kristin Neff, is treating oneself with the same kindness one would show a friend while dealing with adversity, failure, or the realisation of an unattractive trait. She goes so far as to say that it's "healing ourselves with love." Self-compassion is defined by Dr Chris Germer as a "warm-hearted attitude of awareness when we suffer, fail, or feel inadequate," which is borne up by his corpus of research.

Self-compassion, in contrast to placing one's own needs last, emphasises one's inner connection with oneself and the desire to relieve one's own pain and suffering.

To practice kindness towards oneself seems to be common sense. Being kind, sympathetic, and understanding with ourselves? Count us in! So why is it so hard to change the story and show kindness to ourselves?

Self-compassion, on the other hand, may often look egotistical, self-pitying, or selfish, despite the fact that being compassionate towards others is generally seen as beneficial.

It's tempting to agree with that pessimistic line of thinking, but it's not grounded in reality. Though self-compassion requires an inside gaze, it is one that is less subjective and more attentive than other forms of introspection. Instead of dwelling on our own emotions and ideas, we should work to foster forward motion. The act of focusing on and appreciating one's own strengths is a very beneficial and healthy one.

No one should be too weak to practice self-compassion. It forces us to re-evaluate our assumptions and might reawaken distressing memories. Yet facing this aspect of ourselves may be a healthy long-term healing strategy.

The Upsides of Self-Compassion Practice

Self-compassion is gaining popularity because, like being compassionate to others, it has many positive effects on one's mental and physical health.

Anxiety, sadness, and ruminating have been shown to decrease with self-compassion training. As a result, we are able to develop stronger bonds with ourselves and others via a shared understanding of our shared experiences.

The practice of self-compassion may boost your motivation, sense of self-worth, happiness, general contentment, hope for the future, and resilience, among other positive outcomes.

Self-Compassion: The Three-Part Process

Keep in mind three principles of self-compassion on your path forward.

1.   Self-compassion versus self-criticism

When we fail to meet our own expectations or make a mistake, it's tempting to be quite hard on ourselves. The practice of self-compassion helps us accept our own and the world's inherent frailties. Realising that we all have hardships allows us to treat ourselves with kindness and compassion rather than harsh criticism while we're going through tough circumstances.

2.   Humanity as a whole versus being on your own

To be human is to experience pain. Each of us will endure pain in our own unique way, but it's pain, nevertheless. It's easier to show compassion for ourselves and others when we know this is something we share with other people. The global impact of the 2019 COVID-19 pandemic is a prime illustration of this phenomenon.

3.   Being present versus embellishing

Finding a happy medium between bottling up and overdoing our feelings is another skill necessary for self-compassion. To avoid being mired in our bad feelings at this time, we must first acknowledge them and then put them in context.

Learning to Be Kind to Oneself

Even if you already consider yourself a caring person, it may take some time and effort to develop the ability to show compassion to oneself. We must be patient with ourselves and keep in mind that we, like everything else, are works in progress. Self-compassion is a skill that can be honed with time and effort, allowing us to lead happier, more satisfying lives.

Realising that your efforts to cultivate self-compassion won't magically eliminate negative emotions is the first step. Eventually, you'll be able to embrace your emotions and discomfort and use that acceptance to help you get through them. However, suppressing them will make the situation much more dire.

1. Become more self-aware by cultivating a mindfulness practice.

Mindfulness and self-compassion go hand in hand because they both encourage introspection and help us make sense of our emotional and mental experiences. This permits us to strike a happy medium between friendliness and compassion. It aids in the non-judgmental acceptance of the here and now and in letting go of attachment to outcomes.

The insights you get from practicing mindfulness will have far-reaching positive effects on your state of mind. While the specifics of one's mindfulness practice may vary from person to person, some common entry points include brief guided meditations, journaling, and breathing exercises. You'll start to see the good and bad ways in which your innermost beliefs, sentiments, and wants have been shaping your existence.

2. Confirm your beliefs.

It may seem ridiculous to say encouraging things to yourself when you're having a bad day, but you'll find that doing so is just as comforting as someone else saying them. Some examples are as follows:

"Please don't worry about me right now, honey."

"I am safe."

"Now comes a time of pain. Sadly, pain is inevitable. It is my hope that I would treat myself gently. I pray I have the kindness to show myself."

"When it comes to me, I am soft and considerate."

"To myself I provide tender, loving care."

"For once, I will be kind to myself."

3. Consider how you would treat a close friend.

Whenever self-criticism arises in the future, just remind yourself, "Would I speak to [insert friend's name] this way?" It's quite unlikely that you would. How would you feel if you tried talking to yourself in the same manner you would talk to another person?

4. Allow yourself to be human and make mistakes.

We've established that flaws and pain are inherent to the human condition; know that you're not alone in this. When we give ourselves permission to make mistakes, we give ourselves the chance to feel more at ease and have more genuine experiences.

5. Make a note to yourself.

Send a heartfelt letter of encouragement to your adult self or your younger self. Just tell yourself that you're OK and that everything is fine and list all your best traits.

Here are five other things you must do to improve your capacity for self-compassion by drawing on your strengths and those of the world around you.

1. Make an effort to forgive others.

Quit being so hard on yourself. Recognise your humanity and be kind when you're reminded of your flaws. It is not because you are perfect that your friends and co-workers like you so much, but rather they appreciate you for who you are.

Learn to recognise the situations in which you have attached your feeling of self-worth to your level of achievement. Realise that no characteristics must be met before a person may love them.

A sticky note with a message telling you to be patient and friendly to yourself, even if you aren't doing well, may be kept near a desk or in a wallet as a constant reminder that you are worthwhile.

There's no use in reserving punishment for the future on account of the present. Get over it by forgiving yourself, learning from the experience, and letting go.

2. Have an open mind and strive for improvement.

Carol Dweck's work is on how our outlook affects our happiness. According to her research, the difference between having a fixed and a progressive mindset may be felt in our level of contentment. The use of a development mentality is more beneficial. Consider difficulties, insurmountable roadblocks, or exciting new adventures.

It's better to face adversity head-on than to try to escape it. When you criticise yourself and negatively compare yourself with others, try to find inspiration in their successes and strengths instead of feeling threatened.

3. Show your appreciation.

Strength comes from enjoying what we have right now rather than pining for what we do not. As we count our blessings, we quiet the critical voice within and shift our attention from ourselves to the beautiful world around us. Keep a thankfulness notebook or take regular gratitude walks, whatever you choose.

4.   Find the right level of generosity.

Those who give the most are themselves the most generous, and this is because showing kindness may be accomplished in many ways. The world indeed needs more givers, but those who consistently put the needs of others above theirs run the risk of being miserable.

Selfless giving is necessary for it to benefit the recipient. To succeed at generosity, you must first know your limits. Then deliberate how you use your time, money, and other resources to benefit your well-being.

Furthermore, enjoy the benefits of your generosity. Learn from the impact you've made and remember to reward yourself. Giving to others improves our sense of well-being only if doing so has no adverse effect on our lives.

5.   Maintain your awareness.

Practicing mindfulness, which tends to lessen self-judgment, has improved self-compassion. To cultivate self-compassion, focus on being present and aware of the here and now without attaching meaning to it.

Don't shout your feelings from the rooftop or bury them in the closet; give them their due time and attention. So let them in and then release them without holding on to them.

CHAPTER ——————————————— 3

Master Your Emotions

E motions are not simple states but include physiological and cognitive shifts, which have consequential effects on our disposition and actions. There is a direct correlation between the experience of an emotion and a corresponding physical reaction: tears of joy or sorrow, a racing heart in response to fear, or a flushed face from rage. Involvement of emotional mastery occurs at the behaviour stage. After then, we adjust our actions to match how we're feeling. We may embrace, flee, or get into a fistfight with another person. Knowing how to control our feelings allows us to stop negative emotions before they cause negative actions.

Beyond this description, there are other ideas about the origins of emotion and the factors that influence our reactions to certain stimuli. Emotions are undeniably potent and must always be considered.

What exactly is emotional mastery?

Emotional mastery has been defined in many ways throughout the last century, as reported by *Psychology Today*. The James–Lange Theory, widely accepted in early American psychology, claimed that emotions are entirely biological in origin (a neurological response to some external stimuli). This perspective was developed when the Cannon–Bard Theory proposed that the thalamus is a mediator between environmental cues and an individual's internal emotional state.

It wasn't until the Schachter–Singer experiment of the 1960s, in which participants were given a placebo vitamin, that the idea of emotional mastery was formally presented. The next step was for everyone to observe their co-workers as they filled out questionnaires. The participants experienced anger when their co-workers replied angrily to the surveys. On the other hand, the participants' moods improved when their co-workers reacted positively. The findings suggested a link between social pressure and emotional experience.

Allen Beck, a psychiatrist, expanded on the notion that one's emotional state is shaped not just by one's ideas and experiences but also by those of one's peers and external circumstances. The cognitive behavioural therapy that is now considered the gold standard for emotional mastery was developed mainly due to Beck's research.

The value of knowing how to control one's emotions is best shown by asking why.

Our subjective experience of the world, or the way we perceive the things that happen to us, is influenced by our feelings and our ability to control our emotions, in contrast to our objective experience, which is the facts we know. Because of this, psychologists agree that one characteristic of emotions is their capacity to shape our judgments and decisions.

Our subjective impressions are immutable. Inevitable events occur daily that we can't prevent or prepare for. Our personal experience, however, is malleable; the significance we ascribe to external events is within our control. That emotional intelligence at work has far-reaching consequences for our relationships, sense of self-worth, capacity for effective communication, and contentment with life.

Traditionally United by Our Feelings

Happiness, sorrow, fear, anger, surprise, and disgust are the six core emotions shared worldwide. Although cultural norms around expressions of emotion vary, we can all relate to experiencing similar sentiments.

Our Feeling of Well-Being Is Controlled by Our Emotions

Considering that our feelings arise from our experiences and the meanings we assign to those events, it stands to reason that we might train ourselves to feel better by doing the opposite. We may prepare ourselves for a positive self-image by practicing humble gratitude, passion, love, hunger, curiosity, confidence, adaptability, cheerfulness, energy, and a sense of contribution. To develop emotional mastery and lay a foundation of good affect, there are ten "power emotions" to choose from.

Prosperous Relationships Rely on Emotional Mastery

Exhibiting the right feelings at the right time is a powerful tool for developing and maintaining meaningful connections. When you lack emotional intelligence, you may lose your cool over trivial irritations or respond angrily when grief is more suitable. People around you will feel and react to your emotions, positively or negatively impacting your relationships.

The moment to deal with emotion is when you feel its full force. Therefore, it will no longer keep resurfacing. Feeling in charge of your feelings and life is within your reach if you follow these six simple steps:

1. Get in touch with your genuine emotions.

To learn how to control your emotions, you must first recognise them. If you want to get control of your feelings, at this moment, ask yourself,

> What am I truly feeling?
> Should I trust these feelings?
> Could there be another explanation?

2. Acknowledge and appreciate your emotions since you can count on them to help you.

Acquiring emotional control does not entail being emotionally numb. Instead, gaining dynamic control requires accepting your feelings as a fundamental part of who you are.

3. Your feelings should never lead you astray.

Convincing yourself that your feelings about anything are "wrong" is a terrific technique to shut off open lines of communication with yourself and others. Consider what this feeling could be trying to tell you and feed your curiosity.

When you've mastered your emotions, you treat them with the same interest you'd show a stranger. Giving in to your feelings will reveal a wealth of information about who you are.

4. Curiosity helps in several ways.

Stop the cycle of surface you're in right now.
Get through the difficulty.
Avoid repetition of this mistake in the future.

5. Take pride in yourself.

When you reflect on a moment when you had a comparable emotion and managed it well, you get instant and tremendous emotional control. Since you overcome the feeling before, you should be able to do it again.

Ensure that you can deal with this situation not just now but also in the future.

Developing self-assurance and competence in managing emotions requires practicing responses to potential triggers. Imagine yourself successfully navigating the scenario visually, aurally, and tactilely.

This emotional analogy of weightlifting will help you develop the "muscle" you need to deal with your emotions.

6. Get enthusiastic and do something.

If you've recently mastered the art of emotional regulation, you should celebrate the fact that you can now do the following:

- ❖ Competently manage your emotions
- ❖ It would help if you did something right immediately.
- ❖ Show that you can manage it by doing so

To live a simple and satisfying life, one of the most valuable skills you should acquire is the ability to control your emotions.

Emotions are not simple states but include physiological and cognitive shifts which have consequential effects on our disposition and actions. There is a direct correlation between the experience of an emotion and the corresponding physical reaction: tears of joy or sorrow, a racing heart in response to fear, or a flushed face from rage.

Involvement of emotional mastery occurs at the behaviour stage. After then, we adjust our actions to match how we're feeling. We may embrace, flee, or get into a fistfight with another person. Knowing how to control your feelings allows you to stop negative emotions before they cause negative actions.

Beyond this description, there are other ideas about the origins of emotion and the factors that influence our reactions to certain stimuli. Emotions are undeniably potent and must always be considered.

Control Your Emotions; Don't Let Them Control You

When you look back, do you find yourself regretting what you said in a fit of rage? Do you allow your fears to prevent you from taking chances that may improve your life? If this describes you, know that you're not alone.

Feelings have a great deal of influence. How you feel affects every aspect of your life, from the relationships you cultivate to the resources you allocate to the difficulties you face.

If you can learn to rein in your emotions, it will help you develop a more robust mind. Fortunately, improving one's ability to control their emotions is a skill that can be learned. Emotional control is a talent like any other, requiring time and effort to develop.

Feel the Painful Emotions, But Don't Dwell There

Emotion management is not the same as emotion suppression. Not dealing with your feelings of melancholy or pretending you are not experiencing pain will not make them go away.

In fact, time usually makes emotional wounds worse if they aren't treated. Suppressing emotions may lead to the employment of harmful coping mechanisms, such as overeating or drinking.

It's healthy to be in touch with your emotions, but remember that you're not at the mercy of them. If you get out of bed on the wrong side of the bed, you have the power to change your outlook on life. You have the ability to control your anger.

Here are three strategies for regulating your emotions:

1.   Give feelings names

Realising how you're really feeling is the first step in altering that feeling. Can you describe your level of anxiety? Aww, are you sad now? Do you feel sad?

It's important to remember that anger may serve as a shield for more delicate feelings, such as guilt or humiliation. Focus on your inner experience and take it seriously.

Indicate how you really feel. It's important to remember that it's normal to experience a range of feelings, from anxiety and frustration to irritability and impatience.

Putting a name to your feelings might make them seem less overwhelming. In addition, it may help you keep in mind the potential impact your emotions have on the choices you make.

2. Recast your approach

Feelings colour your judgment. If you're feeling nervous and your employer sends you an email saying she needs to see you immediately, you could believe she intends to dismiss you. If, on the other hand, you're in a good mood when you receive the email, you could assume that you've just been promoted or commended for a job well done.

Consider the slant of your emotions as you see the environment. Next, reorganise your thinking to form a more practical perspective.

The moment you realise you're thinking "Attending this networking event is pointless. No one will speak to me and I'll appear like an idiot," tell yourself, "It's up to me to get something out of the event. When I meet someone new, I'll introduce myself and ask questions about them."

Asking yourself "What would I say to a buddy who had this problem?" will give you some distance and help you see things more objectively. Providing an answer to that question can help you think more logically by removing some of the emotion from the situation.

If you find yourself fixating on the bad, it may be time to switch mental channels. Stopping yourself from ruminating might be as simple as getting up and moving around for a while.

3. Take part in a mood-raising activity.

When you're feeling down, it's more likely that you'll do things that hinder you from feeling better. Bad mood habits include isolating yourself, compulsively browsing through your phone, and moaning to others around you.

But they will block you from moving forward. If you want to feel better, you need to do something about it.

Consider the actions you do while you're feeling joyful. If you want to feel better while you're feeling down, try doing those activities.

Some things that may lift your spirits are listed below.

- Get in touch with a friend and have a nice chat (not to continue complaining).
- Take a stroll around the neighbourhood.
- Take a few minutes to meditate.
- Play some music that makes you feel better.
- Maintain your efforts to regulate your emotions.
- Emotional regulation might be difficult at times, and there's bound to be one feeling, like rage, that occasionally takes over.

However, the more effort you put into controlling your emotions, the more robust your mind will become. You'll learn to trust in your resilience in the face of adversity, and you'll feel empowered by the knowledge that you have the power to alter your mood through positive lifestyle choices.

CHAPTER 4

Humour When Facing Adversity

People who can bounce back from adversity often have a good sense of humour. Resilient people look back on their hardships and chuckle about them. A positive outlook can help us persevere through difficult times. Moreover, it prevents us from dwelling on problems. An optimistic outlook allows us to take in the good and the bad in any given scenario.

Mental resilience is a reasonably constant personality feature, and studies have shown that maintaining a positive outlook can aid in developing this "hidden strength." Therefore, being resilient is not automatically associated with having a pleasant mental state. The opposite is true; experiencing pleasant feelings during difficult times might aid in coping.

Laughter should not be taken lightly. It's one of our oldest and most valuable natural resources, and it has to be protected at all costs.

Humour and health

To alleviate tension, ease pain, and resolve disagreements, all one has to do is smile. Nothing can help us get back on our feet any quicker or better than this. Laughter helps us feel better, gives us hope, brings us together, and keeps us awake and focused.

Feeling optimistic amid hardship also has a physiological effect. Humour has been linked to various immune-enhancing effects, including higher salivary levels of immunoglobulin A. An essential antibody, immunoglobulin is a protein. It is the first line of protection against respiratory illnesses.

Taking a humorous outlook on hardship has also been linked to a quicker recovery from physical ailments. In addition, it decreases the reoccurrence of illnesses that need hospitalisation among the elderly. Among its many other advantages is a reduced need for inpatient care.

One of the most effective tools you possess for ensuring that your everyday mood and mental state are conducive to good health is your sense of humour.

Optimistic individuals do better in difficult situations

When hardship strikes, one may either develop or wither away. A positive mental outlook is critical. Optimistic individuals decide to build themselves. Many people may need help grasping this. Changing your mindset and confronting misfortune head-on is more complex but achievable.

"Man may be taken away from everything but one: the last of the human rights, the option of the particular attitude he must adopt towards his fate to establish his path," Viktor Frankl stated in his book *Man's Search for Meaning*. Remember that Frankl spent years in a Nazi concentration camp, and the words have a new meaning.

As Nietzsche put it, a man with a purpose in life can persevere through practically anything. When we have a goal in sight, we also have a well from which to draw strength. People who are content with their lives can laugh in the face of hardship and look on the bright side of life. They can maintain concentration.

Many worries and dislikes are associated with prosperity, and many comforts and hopes are related to hardship.

Despite facing challenges, we can still achieve success. There is hope, and together, we can conquer and develop, becoming more than we ever imagined we could be. In several studies, happiness has been found to lead to success in the face of adversity. They don't get stranded, and they use hope to progress despite the storm. You should be able to if they can.

Peace in chaos

If you could find calm in the midst of disarray, what would you do?

You may have to cope with a plethora of survival brain triggers on a daily basis, each of which may cause a cascade of feelings, thoughts, and bodily sensations that may make even the most routine of tasks seem frantic or out of your hands.

For you, what does total anarchy look like?

Is it stressful to keep up with conflicting news stories on social media? Your kids keep interrupting your video conference while you're trying to talk to your partner, who is also working from home. Or you're attempting to make a number of choices while facing substantial uncertainty.

Disarray may also manifest on the inside. Perhaps you're experiencing a dull discomfort in your head, neck, or back. Perhaps you can't go to sleep because your mind won't stop racing, replaying the events of the day or going over your to-do list for the following day.

It may be difficult to find even fifteen minutes a day to meditate, let alone ten days, or take time off for a quiet retreat. To help you find calm in the midst of the storm, here are three easy strategies:

> Muscles get most of the attention, but our organs need work too.

> Keep your legs shoulder–width apart, tap your gut softly (about two inches down from your belly button) with your fists, and visualise the vibrations traveling through your body's centre. The sacral chakra, or the second chakra, is a vital energy point in your body associated with the process of giving birth.

Try closing your eyes and letting your thoughts wander. Tune in to the place in the heart of your being where the vibration is the strongest.

Put your attention and your energy will follow. Light, sound, and vibration are all forms of energy transmission. The vibrations in this practice are meant to help you focus on your own physical centre.

After about a hundred taps with your fist, squeeze your abs in towards your spine as you're doing a crunch while standing or sitting up. Don't let up on the gas. Colon hydrotherapy is the term for this kind of activity.

Having employed vibration via tapping, you have drawn the energy that had been floating about your head down to your abdomen. Exercises that target the intestines are excellent for stimulating internal body heat and maintaining a focal point on the digestive tract.

We tend to act on our emotions rather than our rationale. Using the "water up, fire down" theory, you may reverse this asymmetrical flow of energy and warm your core from the "fire" in your brain while cooling your mind with the energy from your stomach.

When you work out your digestive system, you improve your "water up, fire down" circulation by pumping new oxygen, improving blood flow, better absorbing nutrients, and digesting undigested waste. Heat production, perspiration, and salivation are all signs of healthy blood flow.

Get control of your feelings

Accepting and even embracing negative feelings like anger, despair, or envy may be very helpful in other exercises that aim to teach you how to gain control of your emotions.

Even if you just have five minutes, you may use that time to practice being detached from and monitoring your emotions. Here's an example of one activity that has been really effective for my business leader clients.

Put your head down and your eyes closed. Look over your whole body from head to toe. Where do you feel stress, discomfort, or negative feelings the most?

A good question to ask oneself is "What colour is the pain or undesirable emotion? To what form does it take? To what feel do you refer? What's the deal with that ruckus?"

Take a moment to recall a joyful experience. Look at your company. Where are you? What kinds of sounds and aromas are in your environment? To what extent do you sense it?

Let the positive emotion of that recollection permeate your whole body

So please feel the anguish once again. Your pain may be different colours at different times, so you may want to ask yourself, "What colour is it currently? To what form does it take? To what feel do you refer? What's the deal with that ruckus?"

Many people who put this into practice report that unpleasant feelings change form, intensity, and even vanish completely.

The sooner you can build emotional resilience as a leader, the greater your potential as a leader.

The internal audience

Meditation on the self is the last step towards serenity.

All you have to do is shut your eyes, take a few deep breaths, and then ask your heart, "What's my message for today?"

Maintain your line of inquiry and attentive listening. Quite often a brief reply will do.

Any organ or painful location may benefit from verbal communication, not only the heart.

If you learn to listen to your inner knowledge, you'll be able to make choices that are right for you and your life without second-guessing or feeling regret.

When you train regularly, your mind, body, and heart become more in sync, allowing you to easily observe fleeting thoughts, feelings, and body sensations rather than becoming engulfed by them.

For true mastery, regular effort is necessary

Finding calm requires first centring one's attention inside, away from the world. Then channel that power deep into your body. Your whole being (physically, emotionally, mentally, and spiritually) is now in harmony, and it only took a few minutes.

You may strengthen your internal compass to help you make better decisions in times of doubt by turning within. No matter how crazy things become, whether inside or out, you'll be the one who keeps everyone sane. In each given situation, you get to choose the action that best fits the scenario.

If you have the fortitude to cultivate stillness through moving meditations, emotional regulation, and introspective awareness, you will not only find calm in the midst of chaos but also contribute to the calming of the world around you.

Being the embodiment of calm in the midst of upheaval allows you to tap into an endless well of strength for the benefit of your team, clients, investors, and most of all, yourself.

CHAPTER ——————————— 5

Engage in Wellness Activities

As we go on the road to mental health and wellness, let's pause to address and bring to light a topic that is crucial to our well-being but often overlooked: spirituality. While most of us go about our days in an automated fashion that we've constructed and accepted, we whine about the boredom of our routines and do little to change them. This jolt will contribute to our overall mental health. It will have far-reaching consequences if we don't break out of this rut or inject some excitement into our daily lives.

Activities such as school, reading, learning something new, playing a sport, watching a movie, etc., are ingrained in us from a young age. When we become involved in anything, it's because it's something we like doing or have strong feelings about. The question then becomes why, as we age and join the corporate or professional sphere, we fail to remember or no longer consider it vital to devote time to such activities to further our knowledge and development.

Worthwhileness of education

What will you do to stay afloat and ahead of the competition in today's world?

It is natural to believe that after we have graduated from college and entered the workforce, we can begin putting our acquired knowledge into practice. Because of the time constraints imposed by this activity, we often need to pay more attention to pursuing other educational opportunities. The moment we feel the bad effects of this mindset, we decide to snap out of it and do something about it. So as not to become obsolete, you need to commit yourself to a lifelong process of learning and discovery.

If you're like most people, you've probably caught yourself comparing yourself to others at least once. While this might be a healthy dose of motivation to study, it also carries the risk of causing unnecessary anxiety if you aren't up to the challenge. So why not compete and compare yourself to your past, current, and ideal future self? If you do this, you'll know how much and what knowledge you want to acquire.

After that, avoid becoming complacent even if you've absorbed all the relevant information. Don't settle for less.

To what extent does one's level of intelligence influence one's health?

To improve one's intelligence and originality, one must be open to new information and capable of picking up new abilities such as analysis and problem-solving.

Numerous studies and investigations at the national and international levels have shown that this area needs to be more frequently addressed, particularly after the student years are over. Mental and professional health has suffered as a result of this. Focus switches from lifelong learning and improving one's skill set to making more money and climbing the corporate ladder when one moves from college to the working world. While this is essential, participating in intellectually oriented activities also improves your abilities and self-confidence, keeps you aware of the world around you, and keeps you updated on current events. Maintaining a state of cognitive activity benefits your health in all three realms. Reading, writing, problem-solving (including puzzles), following a hobby, traveling, and so on are all examples of such pursuits.

Reading the following summary, you can learn more about your options for achieving intellectual wellness. The four main ones are as follows:

1. Develop proper routines in your life

Your routines will shape who you are and what you want to become. Your mental and emotional energy will be high if you pursue a challenging goal. Reading regularly is an excellent way to expand your lexicon and sharpen your grammar, syntax, and prose for adequate expression. It's also helpful to surround yourself with individuals who push you to improve. Meet individuals who know more than you do and can help you grow.

Even if you only have time for one movie or one episode of a TV series, make it a point to choose something that will teach you something new. Inculcate such habits that will keep you motivated and at the same time provide you time off to enjoy yourself and stay abreast of cultural developments.

Keeping oneself energised is crucial at the end of the day. Even though it seems tedious at first, you can enjoy it after you realise its benefits. The following will not provide the desired outcomes if they are performed out of a sense of obligation or burden.

2. Maintain your energy levels

Keep your curiosity and energy for learning high at all times. We all have periods of low confidence and reluctance to engage in conversation. Both our private and professional lives may benefit from this realisation. Attending a forum, even if you cannot participate in it, will allow you to pick up valuable information on a wide range of subjects. Knowing more about the things that interest you makes it simpler to have discussions that go somewhere useful. Talking about meaningless things won't help you learn more or become smarter.

Reading is a great way to expand your lexicon and learn how to express yourself clearly and concisely. This will improve your ability to express yourself verbally and in writing. You understand that good communication is crucial. In this case, language is secondary. Your intended message and audience will determine the best approach. Your communication style also helps you find solutions to issues at home and in the workplace.

Instead of always looking to other people to fix issues, try solving them yourself. It's good for you since it will get you out of your comfort zone and make you use your brain to find a solution. That's a sure way to maintain your energy levels and enthusiasm. Is it possible to live a trouble-free existence? It would be wonderful if it were feasible.

You wouldn't sit back and relax if you were being taxed. Nevertheless, the truth is different. Therefore, it's essential to take preventative measures rather than react. Alternatively, you may put on your thinking and creative hat and attempt something new.

3. Try something fresh

The term "new things" may either refer to completely novel endeavours or be used to describe attempts to approach normal activities in novel ways. Which do you prefer: setting or following the latest fads? Your goal should be to find possibilities if you wish to be a setter. Plan, investigate, learn, try, and apply. The result may not be what you hoped for, but you may take heart that you tried something new regardless of the outcome.

Instil in yourself the ability to think of and implement novel solutions. The pursuit of every interest or pastime requires some degree of originality. Musicians often experiment with different songs, lyrics, and instruments to improve their craft. Similarly, you may enrol in seminars, courses, etc., to learn, practice, and ultimately apply more significant originality and innovation in your chosen sector. For your happiness, fulfilment, and development as a person, as well as your mental health, it is essential to keep your mind active and engaged.

4. Keep your mind open to new information

It's essential to consider the value you'll get from trying something new and whether it fits in with the current cultural milieu. Whether in your field of expertise or your general interest, being abreast of the latest trends and knowing what's happening around you is essential. You need to do more than decide to stay current. To benefit from them, you must include them in your daily routine.

You may have to learn some new abilities to do this. It's great if you already have such talents, but you shouldn't assume that's the case. It's exciting to acquire new knowledge. It boosts self-assurance and makes you feel like you can take life by the horns. These are all positive outcomes of learning new talents. You may take on greater responsibility and more advanced tasks in life if you're constantly improving and expanding your skill set.

Various resources online and elsewhere may help you achieve your goals, including training programs, courses, and even do-it-yourself techniques. You may feel pressured to take on too much. For this reason, be picky about the things you let into your life; they should have a purpose and interest you.

Keep in mind that learning is something you should constantly be doing.

The importance of physical fitness

Exercising is beneficial for you, but how? Discover the many ways in which exercise may enhance your life, from your mental health to your intimate relationships.

Want to improve your health, increase your vitality, and maybe even extend your life span? Only work out.

It's impossible to dispute that maintaining a regular exercise and activity routine is beneficial to your health. Exercise is beneficial for people of all ages, sexes, and levels of physical ability.

Still need more evidence to start acting? Here are seven ways in which regular exercise may improve your life and health.

Exercising is the first line of defence against weight gain.

Exercising regularly can aid in avoiding or keeping off unwanted weight gain. Calories are dissipated in the process of working out. More energy is used in proportion to the intensity of the activity.

Go to the gym on a regular basis, but don't stress if you can't devote a significant portion of each day to training. As opposed to doing nothing, even a little bit of exercise may help. Get more active in your day-to-day life, such as by taking the stairs instead of the elevator or by increasing the pace at which you do household tasks, and you will experience the health advantages of exercise without having to commit to any formal exercise program. Be consistent.

Health problems and illnesses may be fought off by regular exercise.

Are you concerned about cardiovascular disease? Aiming to stay away from hypertension? Physical activity increases high-density lipoprotein (HDL) cholesterol, the "good" cholesterol, and reduces harmful triglycerides, regardless of your current weight. These two measures work in tandem to maintain your blood flowing freely, which lowers your chance of cardiovascular disease.

By maintaining a regular exercise routine, you may reduce your risk of or effectively treat various health issues, such as

- stroke
- chronic hypertension
- recurrent insulin resistance and type 2 diabetes
- depression/anxiety

- It reduces the chance of mortality from any cause and has been shown to boost cognitive performance.
- Exercising boosts your spirits.

Do you need a pick-me-up? Is today particularly hectic, and you might use some time to unwind? Try going for a jog or exercising at the gym. Many people report increased feelings of contentment, calmness, and reduced anxiety after engaging in physical exercise.

If you exercise consistently, you may also experience an increase in confidence and a lift in self-esteem because of the positive effects on your perception of your physical self.

It boosts energy levels.

Tired after doing errands or food shopping? Strengthen your muscles and increase your stamina with a regular exercise routine.

Exercising increases the efficiency of your cardiovascular system by delivering oxygen and nutrients to your tissues. When your heart and lungs are healthier, you'll have greater stamina for mundane tasks.

Regular exercise leads to greater sleep quality.

Is it hard for you to fall asleep? You may improve your sleep quality, fall asleep more quickly, and experience deeper sleep if you engage in regular physical exercise. If you want to avoid being too energetic to fall asleep, avoid exercising just before bed.

As a result of regular exercise, your sexual life will once again be exciting and exciting.

Do you feel too worn out or unfit to take pleasure in physical contact at the moment? Maintaining a regular exercise routine has been shown to raise both energy and self-esteem, both of which are positively correlated with an individual's libido.

However, there is more to it than that. Women who exercise regularly may experience more arousal. Men who engage in regular physical activity have a lower risk of erectile dysfunction than their less active counterparts.

It's possible to enjoy physical activity while interacting with others.

Physical activity and exercise can be fun. They provide an opportunity to relax, take in the scenery, or do whatever makes you happy. Getting your body moving is a great way to spend quality time with your loved ones, whether it be your family or your friends.

Do something active like enrolling in a dance class, going on a hike, or signing up for a soccer team. Find something active that you enjoy doing and do it. Bored? Do something different or do something with people you care about.

Ultimately, the conclusion about exercise is . . .

Physical activity and exercise are excellent methods to improve your mood, strengthen your body, and have some fun. The recommended exercises of the US Department of Health and Human Services for most healthy individuals are as follows:

Performing an aerobic routine: Participate in at least 150 minutes of moderate aerobic exercise per week or 75 minutes of strenuous aerobic activity per week or a mix of the two. The instructions recommend breaking this task up into seven daily sessions. Getting at least 300 minutes of exercise each week is suggested for maximum health benefits and to help with weight reduction and maintenance. However, any quantity of physical exercise is better than none. The health benefits of being active for little bursts throughout the day build up.

Conditioning the muscles: At least twice a week, you should engage in strength training that targets all of your main muscle groups. Try to complete one set of each exercise with a weight or resistance level that will weary your muscles out after twelve to fifteen repetitions.

Aerobic activity on a moderate level includes brisk walking, bicycling, swimming, and mowing the yard. Aerobic exercise that is both intense and prolonged includes activities like jogging, laborious yard work, and aerobic dance. The use of weight machines, free weights, body weight, heavy bags, resistance tubing or resistance paddles in the water, and even rock climbing may all contribute to strength training.

You may need to do more moderate aerobic exercise if you want to reduce weight, reach your fitness objectives, or get the full advantages.

If you have any doubts about your fitness level, haven't exercised in a while, or suffer from a chronic health condition like heart disease, diabetes, or arthritis, it's important to talk to your doctor before beginning an exercise routine.

Physical fitness challenges

Consistency in your workout routine is challenging. After all, there are several possible barriers, such as lack of time, boredom, injury, and self-doubt. But you shouldn't let it stop you.

1. Unfortunately, I just don't have the time to go to the gym.

It's not always easy to squeeze in a workout routine. Put some thought into how you spend your time to maximise productivity.

Make time for exercise whenever you can. Don't stress out if you can't fit in a complete exercise. Smaller bouts of activity, even just ten minutes of walking here and there throughout the day, have advantages as well. It's also possible to attempt exercising at work.

Time your alarm clocks. Try waking up thirty minutes earlier twice a week to get in some exercise time, even if your days are jam-packed and your evenings are just as crazy. Once you find that your body responds well to morning exercises, you may gradually increase your frequency.

Walk more and drive less. Leave your car in the farthest parking spot possible or a few streets away and walk.

Toss off the old and welcome the new into your daily routine. Instead of going to the movies every Saturday with your family or closest friend, you can start a new tradition of going on a bike ride, taking a swimming class, or going skydiving instead.

2. Working out is dull for me.

It's only human to become bored with the same exercise routine over and over again, particularly if you're doing it by yourself. While it's true that exercise might be tedious, that's not the case for everyone.

Pick out some fun things to do. In this way, you increase the likelihood that you will continue to remain engaged. Just keep in mind that any movement is better than none.

Make some adjustments to your daily regimen. Alternate between cardio exercises such as walking, swimming, and cycling to train your muscles in a comprehensive manner.

Get in sync. Do your workouts with people you know, such as your family, neighbours, or colleagues. The group's support and companionship will be invaluable to you.

Learn about your alternatives. Master new abilities as you work out your body. Visit a local gym or community centre and sign up for a sports league or group workout class.

3. A common refrain from me during workouts is "I'm so self-conscious about how I appear."

Get off your low horse! Think about its positive impact on your health or how much better you feel after an exercise.

Be wary of the masses. Avoid exercising in a group setting if doing so makes you anxious. Check out some fitness content or a game that encourages physical activity. You may also get some kind of home workout equipment, such as a stationary bike, treadmill, stair climber, or anything similar.

Think ahead. Congratulate yourself for prioritising your health and well-being. Never forget that your confidence will most likely rise in tandem with your fitness and comfort level in the gym.

4. The thought of working out after a long day at the office exhausts me.

Feeling too tired to work out? You won't have any strength if you don't work out. This is a self-perpetuating cycle. One of the nicest things you can do for yourself is to start an exercise routine. Middle-aged parents can exercise while having fun with their kids.

If you want to be in shape, try working out first thing in the morning. Do you recall how we suggested you wake up thirty minutes earlier so that you might get in a workout? Walk, ride a stationary bike, listen to the radio, or watch the news as you get your workout done. Alternatively, you may go for a quick stroll outside.

Do something productive during your lunch break. Keep a pair of shoes for walking at your desk and use your lunch break to get some exercise.

Put together a plan. When working out, it's important to wear loose, breathable clothing and sneakers. Bring them along with you to the store or on the road.

5. "I'm too lazy to exercise."

If the idea of going for a run first thing in the morning is leaving you feeling exhausted, try the following:

Establish sensible goals. If your mental hurdle is too high, you can quit without even attempting. Take a stroll around the neighbourhood to get things going. Don't give up if you feel tired out. The next day, go for another stroll around the neighbourhood. Keep it up, and gradually, you'll no longer feel worn out.

Put your natural tendencies to use instead of fighting them. Schedule your workouts during times of the day when you know you will be more energised or, at the very least, less sluggish.

Plan your workouts as you would a meeting. Schedule time for exercise and let your loved ones know about your plans. Obtain their approval and support by asking for it.

Purge The Clutter

However, just because we have a lot going on in our lives right now doesn't imply we're any more content or happy. Here are twenty tips for streamlining your life and making more room for the things that matter most. Reduce the stress of everyday life and have more time on your hands with these simple tips!

This is why life is so difficult, and a maintainable course of action consists of repeatedly taking a series of baby steps.

Life tends to grow more complex as we go through it. We all have daily to-do lists that include things such as "call that important client," "make that dinner appointment," "pay the bills," and "get the kids off the computer."

As our lives get increasingly cluttered with things to do, we prioritise what we have to do above what we want to accomplish.

In some ways, life may be difficult and stressful. You know sometimes it would be nice to hit the stop button and take a few minutes to relax and regroup (or catch up on housework or your to-do list).

However, this is easier said than done when you feel like you have a million things vying for your attention at once. Let's be honest: it's more complicated to streamline your daily routine.

The Easiest Way to Simplify Your Life

Every aspect of today's society pushes us to go above and beyond: to do more, be more, accomplish more, and spend more. We attempt to cram too much into our days and then wonder why we can't seem to get out of the rut we've gotten into as one day blends into the next.

Those who find themselves in this situation are urged to reflect . . .

What are your thoughts on the days that make up your life?

If you're doing the right things, to what would you instead devote your time?

How do you feel right now? Happy and joyful or uncomfortable and scatterbrained?

There's no need to add more chasing, worry, and aggravation to our already-full plates when we can discover methods to slow down and seek a little space and relaxation.

To simplify your life, you need to zero in on what matters most. Finding shortcuts to completing necessary tasks and freeing time for enjoyable pursuits is the goal.

While I can't say that simplifying your life will make everything easier overnight, it will make things simpler.

Simplify Your Life with These Easy Steps

In this chapter, I'll discuss several methods that have helped me streamline my personal life.

While some recommendations may be implemented immediately, others may need more time. Just try out the ones that sound the most interesting to you!

1. Reduce meal complexity

Review your schedule for the next week once a week to prepare for it. Plan out the week's breakfasts, lunches, and meals for the whole family based on that. Pick out the ingredients you'll need for the meals you've planned, make a list, and then go to the store or purchase online for home delivery when it's most convenient.

2. Minimise clutter and make life easier at home

You and your loved ones rest and rejuvenate in your own home. Clutter and disorganisation at home are stress triggers and time wasters. Consider decluttering your house to make more room, reduce stress, and save time. Here are one hundred items you can eliminate right now to help you start decluttering your home.

3. Streamline your wardrobe

We make many choices, big and small, every day. The question of what to wear each day is among the first. Streamlining and cleaning your closet will make it simpler and faster to get dressed in the morning and make you feel good about what you're wearing. Check out this article on how to organise your closet in ten simple steps to get some pointers on clearing out your stuff, enjoying your clothes, and discovering a style that works for you.

4. Just say no sometimes

Say no if you can when someone asks you to do anything that goes against your morals, your schedule, or your interests. What you do with this time is entirely up to you. Not every no means "no forever." Instead, it may just mean "not today." Always keep in mind that if you agree to something, you must reject something else. Always check in with yourself to see what's more important.

5.   Reduce the amount of paper you have lying about

Get yourself a cabinet, a box, a drawer, or even a folder to store all your paperwork. Use dividers labelled with appropriate headings to file documents according to the topic. Ensure it is kept in a secure location. If you don't need to preserve the original, scan them and store the digital copies in properly labelled folders on your computer or the cloud. Paper clutter may quickly accumulate in a house, so it's essential to go through the documents once a week to either photograph, file, or destroy them. See this article for twenty-five additional strategies to improve your organisation.

6.   Reduce the number of things you own

When we amass too many things, it might seem like it has control over us. It's a burden on our time, our strength, and our emotions. Let's see if we can make your life easier if you're dealing with a lot of clutter.

7.   Simplify your time management

Spending your time carelessly is as simple as wasting water, but your time is priceless. I don't believe we should work nonstop since we all need downtime to rest and re-energise. Using our time is up to us, but it should be productive wherever feasible. Is there anything you can put off or decline to do now, given your current schedule and commitments? Recognise the benefits of fewer obligations and enjoy the more flexibility they provide. You should prioritise your tasks and be more conscious of the minor things you do that waste time. Value your time!

8.   Establish your top priorities

Most of us have responsibilities, such as financial obligations, duties to our own company and family, and/or jobs. There's not much room for anything else in our lives as we try to balance all the responsibilities of today. Focusing your time, effort, and attention on what matters to you in your daily life, your monthly life, and your life as a whole is what we mean when we talk about defining your priorities.

Life can dictate our priorities if we don't set some for ourselves. Take stock of your life and give your full attention to the things that matter to you and are essential to your happiness (not just the tasks on your to-do list). Relax, knowing that you don't have to do "all things," and let go of the things that aren't pressing right now.

9. Reduce financial complexity

To save money:

Go paperless with your bills, set up automatic payments when you can, and make a monthly budget you stick to.

Set aside time each month to review your monthly income and expenses peacefully and without interruption.

Save as much as possible, cut spending, and establish a strategy to pay off any outstanding debt. Simplifying your financial life will make you less likely to lose track of your monthly expenditures or overlook a bill payment because it got lost in the pile of paper. Financing should be simplified.

You should try to streamline your nights by doing the following:

Get into a pattern before bed that helps you relax and recharge. Put forth a little more effort the night before to save time in the morning. Then take some time for yourself to relax and forget about today. Pick some things to do that help you wind down and chill out before bed. Examine this article for tips on turning your bedroom into a peaceful retreat after a long day or establishing a regular nighttime routine that works for you.

10. Streamline your morning routine.

Henry Ward Beecher states that the first hour of the day is crucial. Getting up a bit earlier in the morning has made a huge difference for me. It allows me to relax in peace and quiet with a book or my morning tea. Beecher states that the build is a routine that works for you to get your day off to a good start and reflect your ideals for the day ahead.

11. Make health and exercise easier.

If I keep my goals straightforward, I can achieve them better. When things become unrealistically complex, they lose their appeal. Many things in life may be generalised in a way, but for me, this is especially true regarding my physical well-being. Whenever feasible, select healthy food alternatives and get enough exercise and sleep each day. Reduce your exposure to stressful situations and the things you use to cope with stress, such as smoking and alcohol. No marathon training or fad diets are required. In most cases, the most realistic thing to do.

12. Remove mental clutter.

One who has a lot of things to remember, anxieties, issues, and a lot of ideas and information has a crowded mind. If you need mental and emotional breathing room, read my piece on how to clear your mind. If you clear your head of unnecessary thoughts and feelings, you'll be better able to concentrate on what's essential. There's so much more your brain can do than merely recall the minutiae of everyday life. Put your ideas and to-dos on paper (or in your phone's notes) and give your mind a rest. How you think is crucial if you want to do more.

13. Another crucial aspect of your life is your connections.

We've all been in relationships where we felt like we were doing most of the work or things were generally unpleasant and tiring for both parties. If you want to strengthen your relationship with your spouse, here are some suggestions. Get rid of the people who don't bring out the best in you and don't support, encourage, and love you. Don't be nasty or disrespectful. Instead, focus on keeping the peace in a manner that benefits and honours all parties. Spend your time wisely by cultivating genuine friendships and partnerships that enrich your life.

14. Simplify your self-care routine.

When you have a lot going on, it might be easy to put yourself last. Self-care is typically put off until the last possible moment. Instead, consider easy methods to include self-care into your daily life – no need to go to great lengths or spend a lot of money. Modifying just a few things and taking time for yourself can have a considerable impact.

15. Make joy important.

Everyone experiences highs and lows, but one's outlook dramatically influences one's emotional response. Ultimately, we want you to feel more at peace, liberated, and happy. While simplifying your life is a worthy objective, it is not the final destination. Finding methods to relax and simplify your life allows you to devote more time and energy to the pursuits that matter to you rather than merely the mundane tasks that must be completed.

16. Make household tasks easier for yourself.

Keeping up with my house significantly drains my time and stamina. My house is always clean as we have a housekeeper to unload the pressure of our hectic schedule. My household functions that are left are more smoothly on autopilot because of my efforts to streamline my tasks, simplify my home, and put procedures in place to help us all be tidier and more organised.

17. Reduce the complexity of your everyday life.

How often do you reach the day's conclusion without completing your goals? Do you wish you could be more organised and make better use of your time each day so that you can do all that is needed yet have time for yourself? If this appeals to you, establish some manageable routines that integrate themselves into your day and help you get things done.

18. Do away with the mess that no one can see in your home.

Every person has their interpretation of what constitutes clutter. It might be items you can see and touch or those that could cause you mental and emotional distress or take up valuable mental and emotional real estate. Disorganisation may also take many shapes.

19. Get rid of your negative influences since they are just holding you back.

Think about the positive and negative aspects of your life right now. In what ways do you find inspiration, motivation, and challenge, and what factors drag you down and make you struggle? Improve the areas that need it, take care of the things you can, and learn to let go of the things holding you back (like too much time gaming or chatting on social media and other much more time-wasting activities that will set you back).

Be Grateful

A famous quote from Ferris Bueller says, "Life goes very quickly. You could only notice it if you take a moment to glance around every once in a while."

Being grateful and appreciative are hallmarks of a life well-lived. Sometimes in life's fast lane, it's easy to lose sight of the good things around you. Here are eight suggestions to incorporate more thankfulness into your everyday life and aid you in your gratitude quest.

Don't be fussy. Instead, learn to enjoy the little things.

You shouldn't save your thanks until the significant milestones in your Life. The first step in developing a gratitude habit is realising that no good thing in life is too little to be grateful for.

Take your time with the little things while counting your blessings; for example, be thankful that the mail arrived swiftly last Friday despite the cloudy weather.

Be thankful for your difficulties.

Gratefulness extends beyond just appreciating one's good fortune. It is often through contemplation of adversity that one can better focus on precisely what it is for which they are grateful.

Jack Kornfield, a Western Buddhist teacher, recalls an activity he conducted with a guy taking care of his grandson while his son and daughter-in-law struggled with drug addiction. Despite his hardships, the guy was thankful for the compassion he had developed and the positive effect he had on others' lives.

Try delving into your personal experiences and figuring out how they've shaped you.

1. Train your mind to be present and aware.

Practicing gratitude daily can change your brain's wiring so that you feel happier and more appreciative in everyday life. Take five to ten minutes daily to reflect on the good things in your life. The idea is to create that mental image while simultaneously allowing yourself to experience the thankfulness in your body.

With only eight weeks of regular practice, individuals demonstrate altered brain patterns that ultimately lead to higher empathy and pleasure.

You can make practicing thankfulness easier by teaching your brain to do so. What are you waiting for?

I like the movie *Eat Pray Love* (2010) with Julia Roberts. It reflects all above.

2. Create an attitude of thankfulness by keeping a diary.

If you find yourself thinking only good ideas after practicing mindfulness, record them. Keeping a notebook of your gratitude is a great way to record and reflect on the good things happening in your life.

Putting your optimistic contemplations on paper might help you think about them more intently. Putting pen to paper forces you to give your full attention to the words you are writing at the expense of any other less appreciative ideas that may be vying for your attention at the time.

You can keep a diary and write it daily, weekly, or monthly following your daily thankfulness exercise.

3. Volunteer.

Many individuals have found that volunteering in their community has helped them develop a more grateful attitude. Volunteering for the sake of helping others improves our well-being and hence our capacity to appreciate the things we often take for granted.

That is to say, when you serve others, you benefit yourself.

You might get recognised by others to get your dream opportunity or job.

4. Describe your feelings and thoughts in six words or less.

Being grateful on the inside isn't always enough. To experience more appreciation, show thanks to those who mean the most to you.

As part of their research into the "science of happiness," the Soul Pancake team had participants write gratitude notes to their loved ones. This activity alone boosted their happiness by 2%, reaching 4%. Their happiness levels increased from 4% to 19% when those same folks called the person they were grateful for to express their thanks personally.

In addition to brightening the recipient's day, expressing thanks can do wonders for your sense of thankfulness and pleasure.

5. Devote some of your time to cherished relationships.

Spend time with your loved ones to help you appreciate the present moment and enjoy the good things in your life. It will allow you to bond with them, deepen your connection, and offer you experience in expressing appreciation to those you value.

You could begin with something little if you have difficulty finding methods to help your loved ones. For instance, the next time someone tells you a tale, try really listening to what they have to say instead of waiting for your turn to talk. You can even praise a difficult relative on their new shoes or haircut to get the discussion going.

6.   Find more sources of joy in your life.

Happiness and gratitude go hand in hand; being thankful can bring you joy. Planning an exciting holiday or engaging in a long-awaited activity you like can help lift your spirits. For example, you can take a flying lesson, go skydiving, go to F1 races, or go on a bike ride or a nice long walk.

Once the endorphins start flowing, expressing thankfulness will be much simpler, and you'll find yourself creating gratitude list after gratitude list.

Don't let anyone steal your joy

Don't waste another day feeling down because of other people. People are free to be as impolite and nasty as they choose.

Even if things aren't going as planned, you can still make the most of the day and decide to be joyful. However challenging it may be, you have complete control over your feelings.

Here are some things to keep in mind to guard your happiness from those who would want to destroy it.

Keep your happiness to yourself.

If you want to keep smiling, don't allow anybody to dampen your spirits. It's okay if people are impolite, nasty, and unpleasant.

You can choose to have a good time and an optimistic outlook on life regardless of the circumstances. Despite how it may seem at times, you have complete command over how you feel.

Here are some things to keep in mind to guard your happiness from those who would want to destroy it.

1. You should not allow the rage of others to bring you down.

Many individuals in your life will get upset with you for no apparent cause. At the very least, there's no explanation that involves you.

When other people take their frustrations out on you, it's easy to feel low about yourself. It's not easy to have a cheerful outlook and get through the day despite the distraction.

Yet you are free to decide that you will not allow another person's hostility affect you. If you didn't do or say anything incorrect on purpose, you should simply go on with your day.

People often lash out because they feel they have nowhere else to direct their frustrations.

You may need to actively train your mind to ignore other people's rage on the job, for example. Because not everyone shares your commitment to treating others with compassion and respect, there will be occasions when you need to develop a thick skin.

On the other hand, there are some who share your world because you've invited them there. Saying that being here and interacting with you is an honour is not haughty.

By redefining yourself in this manner, you will learn to treat yourself with the dignity and respect you deserve. You are a privilege, and as such, you get to choose how you want to be treated so that other people may continue to enjoy using you.

A person's access may be restricted if they choose to disobey your rules about who gets to use that service. This is a challenging choice, and I can appreciate that.

Wishing it weren't so, you still have to put this much worth on your happiness so that you don't allow anybody to take it from you. Furthermore, there will be occasions when you are attempting to assist someone and they are upset with you.

Look instead for the meat of the problem. An angry retort will just make matters more tense.

Remember to focus on finding good solutions in what you say. After removing yourself from the source of another person's wrath, you may practice gratitude for the calm that has been restored to your life and redirect your attention to something that makes you happy and gives your life purpose.

2. Don't allow the criticism of others get to you.

This piece of advice is related to the first in some way. Negative words are a common way for individuals to steal another person's happiness.

They lower your self-esteem by talking down to you, insulting you, and generally saying hurtful things. When confronted with adversity, I rely on two main strategies.

First, I don't pay any attention to what others have to say. Why should I care about what someone says about me if they are going to belittle me and treat me with disdain?

Yes, I'm aware that some individuals choose to retaliate and be rude to others who wrong them. Just as the old adage says, I don't feel like responding to it.

In high school, I was often the target of rude comments from my peers, but I learned to ignore them or laugh at the jokes they were making at my expense. I don't have to worry about what others say to me as long as they aren't physically harming me.

This is all because of my second most important strategy for coping with the criticism of others. Suddenly, I realised that I do indeed recognise myself.

I'm aware of my own intelligence and strong work ethic, and I have confidence in my own overall goodness. In general, I think I live and act relatively well. I'm not flawless, and I don't always give my best.

When it comes to your identity, no one knows you better than you do. What everyone believes they know about you is based only on their observations and impressions.

You now have a more well-rounded perspective from which to draw positive and constructive conclusions about who you are. Some individuals have the ability to provide you with insightful comments that are meant to help you grow.

I have no problem with them. Just don't allow somebody to bring you down or make you feel inept by saying things that you should disregard.

Believe in yourself again and again because you are a remarkable person. This will make it less difficult to ignore the cruel and untrue remarks of others.

3. Permit no one to prevent you having fun in life.

In the absence of rage or harsh words, you may have to deal with folks who are always downcast. When you're attempting to relax and take it easy, this might be a major distraction.

You can feel compassion for someone's plight without letting it dampen your own joy. You can keep trying to be encouraging and helpful to assist the other person feel better temporarily. But it's best to spend less time with them if they refuse to lift your spirits or provide anything pleasant.

Another person can't make you happy. Every person is responsible for his or her own happiness.

Don't allow the worries of the day get to you, and don't ever let someone take your happiness away.

You may claim happiness, but you must guard it. It's certain that you'll encounter obstacles throughout your journey through life.

It's OK to let yourself feel sad if you need to. Feel the moment, but don't linger there.

Time is precious, and you should make the most of it by enjoying every moment to the fullest.

How to Deal with Difficult People

It seems like there's always going to be someone trying to be tough, right?

Throughout my professional life, I've often had to deal with challenging clients/employees. It hasn't always been people in my direct environment. Sometimes it's workers or even folks from different teams.

There is also the matter of our families. My own family isn't the only one I've found to be particularly challenging at times. After hearing from many different friends' experiences, I can safely say that many families often push its members to the edge of their sanity.

Don't even get me started on the plethora of individuals we have to engage with at the many businesses we frequent. Whether it's my mobile phone provider or the gardener I hired a year ago, nobody ever shows up when they're supposed to. Nearly four months and weekly follow-ups later, they finally arrived and rectified something that should have been done from the start.

What made you think it would be hard to do that?

Why certain individuals are so challenging to be around is probably not a question with a simple solution. They're as diverse as the individuals who hold them. Being as diverse as we are, it might be surprising how well we get along.

Let's not waste time trying to figure out what makes certain individuals so challenging and instead concentrate on what we have power over: how we respond to them. Let's take a look at some tried-and-true strategies for dealing with thorny situations and individuals.

❖ Show plenty of compassion.

I got it, okay? The natural inclination when dealing with tough individuals is to be harsh yourself. One's natural reaction to feeling threatened is to take up defensive positions. To this day, if I don't stop and take a breath, I may find myself engulfed by the same thing.

In my experience, being polite always gets you further than being demanding does. Nothing productive can come out of a scenario in which two individuals are being tough to each other.

On the other hand, repeatedly using a high volume of compassion towards a challenging individual might help defuse tensions and increase the likelihood that you'll achieve your goals. This is a very effective method for communicating with challenging individuals.

❖ Exhibit kindness.

Have you ever heard the proverb about taking responsibility for yourself? That if you and a large group of other individuals crammed all your issues into a circle, you'd likely take your own troubles back after seeing how bad everyone else's were? As a matter of fact, I adore it.

The point is that none of us can claim to fathom the inner turmoil of anybody else. It's possible that the person being difficult is going through a terrible trial or is attempting to solve a huge issue of which you have no desire to be a part.

Most of the time, a tough individual will react positively if you treat them with kindness. Many of us are preoccupied with our own thoughts and concerns that we fail to notice when others may need a helping hand. When you have a chance, check it out.

❖ Look for a point of agreement.

Have you ever observed that a shared interest or experience might help you bond quickly with a new acquaintance? Having a sense of community and belonging is one of life's greatest rewards. You should always have this excellent skilled method of handling challenging individuals in mind.

It's usually wonderful to meet someone with whom you have a similar college experience. Even though I have two teenage girls now, I used to feel a special connection with other people when I learn that they also have an entrepreneurial and intelligent mindset.

To have a more pleasant discussion with a challenging individual, it might be helpful to locate something that you have in common with them.

❖ Maintain your composure.

Has somebody ever sent you an email at work that made you want to punch them in the face? More often than I want to recall, this has occurred to me.

It's frustrating to have to collaborate on a project with a negative client or employee. I got an email from a tough individual whose whole mission seemed to be making things harder and more confused while I was feeling less than sensible. If I don't take a moment to gather my thoughts, I end up sending an ill-advised email that makes everything much more awkward.

I've found that it usually works out better if I can keep my cool and wait a little time before replying. The ability to maintain composure under pressure is invaluable.

❖ Discuss your point of view.

Just being able to explain to a challenging individual your perspective may make a world of difference.

For instance, it can make a difference if you've hit brick wall after brick wall, and the tough person is your last hope for a resolution.

When faced with a familiar circumstance or topic, some individuals automatically revert to their memorised response. Sometimes it helps immensely if you can share some background information on your current predicament.

You may explain that you've spent the last several months attempting to resolve the issue and that you've already exhausted options X, Y, and Z without success. When this happens, it's often enough to obtain some assistance and unleash the floodgates of compassion. Try it out.

❖ Be respectful while dealing with others.

Nobody I know like being spoken to as if they lack intelligence or ability. Even if someone is being tough, you should always treat them with dignity. You may as well slam the door in someone's face (not really but as a matter of speech) if you start to get upset with them.

When you treat someone badly, they are less likely to help you and may even try to stop helping you altogether. The same principle applies: treat people the way you want to be treated.

❖ Never mind them!

I think it's important to limit or eliminate contact with folks who bring you down. I don't see any reason why I should. They never give me anything except bad advice, and I don't have time for that.

And conversely, avoiding or ignoring a difficult person may be the best option when dealing with them. Of course, it depends on your ability to disregard their existence.

If this is a friend/co-worker you seldom interact with, it may be better to ignore them until they go away.

This also applies to neighbours, certain staff members, and even some customers. It's not always worth it to accommodate a consumer who is being unreasonable. It's not always a terrible idea to let them know that they may be able to find someone else who can help them the way they're hoping to.

❖ Manage what you can.

There are many aspects of life over which we have complete control and just as many over which we have no say whatsoever. Keep your attention on the things you can influence.

Focus on what you can change while dealing with a challenging individual. Is there someone less challenging with whom you can deal? It's possible they're only the beginning of the process.

Recently, I tried to coordinate with the marketing team on a new project I was launching on my own. Whenever I needed assistance, I sought out a certain someone or firm since this was the customary course of action. The individual I emailed ignored my messages. I tried contacting this individual by email and phone numerous times but received no response. After being left hanging, I decided to inquire around to other marketers.

Amazingly, I managed to track down a number of kind and helpful individuals who were all too happy to lend a hand with my undertaking. I cut out the troublemaker. You should exert whatever influence you have on the situation.

❖ Examine yourself.

Looking inside is another of the ten expert tactics for dealing with challenging individuals, like how you're concentrating within. Is there anything you're doing that's making it more difficult to get along with someone than it should be?

For example, I am often in a positive frame of mind. Every day, I spend the majority of my time interacting with other people, and most of these interactions go off without a hitch.

Even while conversing with others, there are occasions when I find myself preoccupied with thoughts and internal problem-solving. When I spend a lot of time thinking rather than talking to other people, I am called arrogant by other people, which is not the case, of course.

In this case, my off-mind comments may only serve to further infuriate someone who is already on edge. My response is just making things worse.

Examine your approach to challenging individuals to make sure you aren't making things worse.

❖ Get over your aversion to confrontation.

One of the most effective methods for coping with challenging individuals is to learn to like confrontation. Being conflict-averse may leave many vulnerable to having more challenging individuals walk all over them.

Setting limits and standing up for yourself may make dealing with a tough person much easier. Everyone, without exception, has a right to be treated with dignity. You shouldn't put up with bad treatment from a thorny individual.

I don't think it's a good idea to provoke people on purpose. What I'm suggesting is that you don't shy away from confrontation if a challenging person is being unfair to you. By not speaking out when they need to, many individuals let others dictate their lives.

Arguments aren't always awful. There are situations when this is beneficial since it paves the way for a satisfactory conclusion: transforming challenges into gains.

Every part of our existence is permeated with challenging individuals. Throughout my career and in my day-to-day life, I've encountered a broad range of individuals and situations, including those where I had to deal with a tough personality or attitude. I'm certain that the next time you're put in a sticky position with a tough person, these ten strategies will come in handy.

Relationship building and communication with others are essential to our survival. Learning how to cope with challenging people can make everyone's lives more pleasant.

CHAPTER ——————— 8

Develop A Growth Mindset

People who have a growth mindset think they can improve their skills and capabilities through time. They believe they can accomplish so by honing their skills via dedicated practice and the accumulation of relevant information.

A fixed mentality, on the other hand, is the conviction that one's strengths and weaknesses are immutable features of their personality. Whether you achieve your goals or not depends on which of these two perspectives you choose. Here are the top 5 reasons why you should adopt a development mindset.

Improves Your Self-Esteem

A development attitude is crucial for self-belief. People who have this sort of perspective will frequently have a realistic assessment of their skills, capacities, and talents to strengthen areas they are strong in and seek to improve areas of shortcomings. They do not give up on their weak areas but strive hard to improve them.

A development attitude encourages people to have confidence that they can accomplish anything if they put in time and effort to study and work. Because of this, individuals are able to do what they could not previously, which boosts their confidence and encourages them to take on even more difficult objectives.

Acquires New Abilities

If you adopt a growth mindset, you will discover that you are more receptive to acquiring new skills and information. If you have a growth attitude, you will work hard to achieve your objectives.

Employers value this trait known as a development mentality when making recruiting decisions. This is because new hires who think they can learn on the job are more likely to put up the effort necessary to acquire the necessary skills and ultimately succeed in their roles.

It's time to take on some new challenges.

In the commercial world, there will always be something new to overcome. These may take various forms, and a business may have to deal with many at once. A hardworking entrepreneur with a development mentality won't whine or give up until the issue at hand is fixed.

In place of assigning blame, a business leader with a growth mentality would encourage teamwork by rewarding those who contribute to the company's success. If they want their teams and employees to believe in themselves and reach their full potential, leaders must embody a growth mentality. While this may be true, it is not a license to engage in reckless behaviour. This suggests you're willing to push the company into uncharted territory by taking calculated risks.

Discover Untapped Potential

When you have a growth mentality, you look for advantages where others perceive disadvantages. It does not imply that you do not identify the problems but rather can assess all the aspects that will make the task a success or a failure. Someone with a closed mentality will give up without even examining other possibilities.

With a development mentality, your mind will unconsciously seek out fresh chances to give rise to novel prospects. However, someone with a fixed attitude won't even try to seize the opportunity since they'll unconsciously assume that they have no chance of succeeding regardless of how hard they try. Boss and employees must have a growth mentality to creatively solve challenges and find new chances to help develop the firm. Hiring specialists should watch out for such persons while staffing a business.

Keep an Eye Out for Opinions

A person with a development mentality is more inclined to solicit criticism in the hopes of refining their approach and outcomes in the future. The reason for this, according to the study's authors, is that when you have a growth mindset, you actively seek out comments as a way to gain insight into a topic from a fresh angle.

People with a fixed mentality see feedback as either unqualified praise or unqualified criticism, and they do not view it as a tool to grow and develop. It's also considered as a way to measure oneself against others, which is counterproductive to development. Having a growth mindset will allow you to evaluate your performance objectively and pinpoint areas of improvement on the job. It doesn't make you feel bad about yourself but rather motivates you to give it another go and become better next time.

A person's mindset consists of their collected ideas and assumptions about who they are. A growth mindset is a conviction that one's abilities may be honed through practice, strategy, and the support of others.

Professor Carol Dweck of the University of California, Berkeley, is widely credited for popularising the concept of a growth mindset in her 2006 book *Mindset: The New Psychology of Success*. Her research aimed to uncover the effect an individual's self-perception of intellect and receptivity to learning had on their output.

In her research, she found that those who think they can improve their skills did better than those who thought their skills were set at birth. Those adopting a growth mindset can look at problems in a new light and choose to push themselves outside of their comfort zone to expand their knowledge.

Professor Dweck describes the phenomenon as follows:

> The idea behind the growth mindset is that you can improve on your most fundamental traits with enough hard work. While everyone is born with unique skills, interests, and temperaments, they may all be honed and expanded through practice and experience.

Understanding that you have the potential to adopt a development mindset is half the work, as this quotation makes very evident:

What's the difference between a growth mentality and a fixed mindset?

A fixed attitude is the polar opposite of a growth one. In contrast to a growth mentality, which emphasises gradual change over time, a fixed mindset is predicated on the assumption that one's talents and skills are set in stone from birth.

People with a fixed mentality think that traits like intellect, ability, and character are given to us from birth.

Those who believe their distinctive traits stem from their DNA are also more likely to think those traits will remain constant throughout their lifetimes.

This kind of thinking is restrictive in some different contexts. Dr Dweck's initial study suggests that people with a fixed mentality are more inclined to actively seek out situations where they may highlight their strengths rather than risk having their deficiencies brought to light.

Furthermore, she argues that such an outlook on life is often counterproductive. People with a fixed perspective may take fewer risks overall, which may cause them to lose out on valuable opportunities and experiences.

Our University of Michigan course The Science of Success delves further into the empirical study of success.

Some research have shown that a student's academic success affects their outlook in a classroom environment. According to the findings, a positive feedback loop connects one's mental attitude with success in the classroom. Is there any truth to the notion that one's intellect may grow?

It has been proven in several studies that a brief online growth mindset intervention may assist in raising academic achievement. The researchers looked at data on math performance and enrolment across secondary schools in the United States to conclude the effectiveness of a short course that teaches that IQ can be cultivated.

However, a study conducted by researchers at the University of Edinburgh found that pupils aged nine to thirteen for whom the growth mindset theory was implemented had no improvement in academic performance. Some have argued that Dr Dweck's initial study is flawed because its findings cannot be repeated or because of statistical bias.

Some have argued that intellect and character are better indicators of academic and professional success. Most notably, in mature individuals, these characteristics tend to be more consistent across time.

But further studies from Dr Dweck and the OECD have shown even more encouraging outcomes. The results from the year 2021 demonstrated that encouraging students to explore new methods of learning and providing constructive criticism may help schools promote a growth attitude.

Students were polled on how much they agreed with the statement "Your IQ is something about you that you can't alter too much." Higher test scores in reading, science, and math were found among those who disagreed (growth mindset) compared with those who agreed (fixed mindset).

Additional investigation into development mindsets and their effects is required. We must learn how to implement and promote such an approach in classrooms and beyond.

People with a fixed attitude may appreciate their efforts and make changes when they feel they have fallen short. You could seek out difficulties, especially if doing so would allow you to expand your knowledge.

The good news is that you can train yourself to adopt a growth mindset if you think it could be beneficial. It's vital to remember that no one has a purely fixed or purely development mentality. Most people fall somewhere in the centre. Here are some practices that might help you adopt a development perspective.

It's also important to remember that not everyone will succeed at every endeavour they undertake. Success can be attained through hard effort, commitment, and attitude, but we all have limits. One's frame of mind does not always determine success. Other circumstances also typically play a larger role.

In light of the above, I have detailed a few strategies for cultivating a development mentality. Some of these are mentioned in our University of Groningen teaching and mentoring open course:

1.   Recognise your current frame of thinking.

You may learn a lot about your present frame of mind by reflecting on your attitude to work or school problems. Consider how often you use phrases like "I'm a natural people person" or "I've learned to work well with people" to describe yourself. Alternatively, you may state that "I earned my way up to the leadership post" or that "I'm a natural leader."

Inquiring about such matters will reveal if you have a more fixed or growing attitude. Understanding this is the first step in making the adjustments that might lead to a new direction in your professional life.

2. Evaluate how much progress you've made on your own.

Why don't you consider a skill that you've honed and become better at over time? What was it that you had trouble with before? Just why is it less complicated now? How did you manage to make such a drastic shift?

The characteristics of a growth mindset are ideas like these which encourage you to reflect on the time and effort you've put into improving in certain areas.

3. Learn from others' cases of achievement.

Think of an example of someone defying the odds and succeeding. Consider their path to achievement and what it says about their growth potential.

4. Find out what people think by polling them.

An innovative strategy to foster a development mentality is to actively seek input from others, regardless of whether or not you feel your effort was successful. This will assist you in establishing targets for development. Depending on the situation, they might help you see where you have grown and still have room to grow.

5. Use the force of "yet."

Part of having a fixed attitude is accepting that there will always be areas where you lack proficiency. You may, however, enhance your abilities in these domains through hard effort and persistence.

The key to adopting a development mindset is realising that your weaknesses are potential strengths you still need to explore.

6. Expand your knowledge.

Do something you've never done before and push yourself to master a skill you're not very adept at. A few good places to begin are the fundamentals of economics, another language, or an instrument.

Having a growth mindset and being more receptive to acquiring new abilities may be fostered by being used to challenging one's established routine.

7. Make mistakes.

Make mistakes and use them as learning opportunities. The initial attempt is seldom successful. Mistakes should be seen as something other than evidence of incompetence but rather as essential building blocks of skill.

Making a mistake is an opportunity to learn about your areas of weakness and get insights into what you still need to know.

8. Treat yourself kindly.

Instead of berating yourself for your mistakes, think about how you'd react if you were in their shoes. How would you respond if someone you knew well failed at something you were an expert in? Would you tell them they were worthless or help them improve?

Practicing mindfulness may enhance your capacity for expression, connection, and empathy. It also helps in the process of recognising and abandoning the stuck mindset-associated ideas.

9. Study existing cases.

It is possible to gain insight from the experiences of others, whether via the teachings of professionals like Dr Dweck or by observing the people around you. It might be instructive to study the habits of individuals who have previously achieved success by adopting a development mindset. Think about how you can use what they do and how they deal with problems in your own life.

10. Aim for the stars, but be practical.

We have seen that several factors contribute to success. Factors such as character, IQ, environment, and experiences all play a role. If you want to succeed, however, you need to give yourself a challenging yet achievable objective.

Although there is significant debate concerning the efficacy of growth mindsets, several studies have shown promising results. Such a mindset might help you grow and learn when coupled with other advantages.

You should be able to use the growth mindset examples and advice we've given to evaluate whether or not adopting this attitude will be useful to your circumstances. You may progress towards your objectives and grow as an individual by pushing yourself to your limits and never stopping your education.

CHAPTER ——————— 9

Cling to Your Purpose

Upon waking up some mornings, you may wonder why you bother living since everything seems pointless.

There are moments when you wish you were a part of something more substantial. You're being drawn in a certain direction, but you just can't put your finger on what it is.

You feel this way because you have yet to discover your true calling.

The question "What am I here for?" does not have a clear or direct answer. It might be like having an epiphany or a sudden realisation.

You may be familiar with the anecdotes of authors and musicians who have known their destinies from birth, the Mozarts of the world who have followed their dreams since they first opened their eyes. You wish, deep in your gut, that you had this "knowing" to propel you ahead.

Assuming you're serious about discovering your life's true calling, you already know a lot of the answers.

The meaning of life: What is it for?

Purpose discovery is associated with increased happiness and well-being on all levels of being. You're looking for a greater depth of flavour, intensity, and zip. In the most basic terms, you want to improve yourself.

You wish you could awaken with a zeal for life you haven't felt since childhood, bursting out of bed with enthusiasm.

You may compare the process of discovering your passion to that of a skilled sculptor, chipping away at the stone to unveil the masterpiece underneath. This masterpiece is your life's work, and it's been waiting for you to uncover it.

The quickest approach to discover how to uncover your purpose is via the art of introspection, which involves delving into the deeper core of who you are to take out the pieces to construct the purpose jigsaw.

Imagine that the "golden thread" of your life leads you to a certain vocation or profession, while for others, it may take the shape of a particular manner of being or expressing yourself.

Think about how this serves your larger goals. If you feel disconnected from the world, finding your reason for being may be the key to reconnecting with something bigger and making a difference in the world.

Even yet, the details of your search for meaning and the "why" behind it may be unique. You'll want this as a safety net before you even get off the ground in case your mind starts to wander. Find it by responding to this inquiry:

> I'm curious as to why you feel the need to investigate the meaning of your existence.

> Jot down or recall whatever that comes to mind. It might be due to any of the factors listed above, or it could be due to something else completely. Keep whatever it is safe and near to you.

The positive effects of discovering your life's true calling

Can you recall a time when you awoke in a completely black room with no way to turn on any lights? Have you accomplished anything of note? That's what it's like to go through life without knowing what you're working for.

Such is the way of life for the vast majority of people. If you want to live a fulfilling life, you must first discover what that purpose is.

The significance of discovering your life's mission and how doing so might enhance your daily experience is outlined below.

What is it in your life that compels you to seek meaning?

This isn't a random post that you clicked on. Perhaps this piqued your interest. As far as I can tell, your curiosity has kept you reading. Therefore, you cannot claim that the reading was random or without significance.

It seems that this post was chosen at random for a click. However, that's not how your brain functions in reality. Put your feet up and reflect on the path that brought you here.

I'm curious as to what sparked your interest in discovering your life's meaning.

When did this matter first catch your attention?

In what ways do you wish your life had more excitement?

Tell me about the recent events in your life that have brought you happiness.

Here are some basic steps to take in identifying and pursuing your unique calling.

✓ To have a reason for living is to have a reason for being.

Knowing why you get out of bed in the morning is essential for maintaining positive mental and physical health and is often the driving force behind stronger relationships. Studies show that only 25% of Americans can honestly say they know why they exist.

In the absence of a driving motivation, daily life may become tedious and devoid of fulfilment. When you discover and embrace your life's true calling, you'll never be the same.

You'll start attracting things you've always desired into your life. Health, riches, and contentment will all be yours. Keep in mind that the first step is always inside yourself. The world around you is a perfect mirror of the one within you.

Having no goals in life will always lead to stress, anxiety, and financial hardship. If you're looking to achieve fulfilment in life, it's important to examine your thought processes and devote some time each day to defining your goals.

✓ You'll get a more in-depth knowledge of who you are.

We are all convinced that we have an intimate understanding of who we are. But very few people have a profound comprehension of who they really are. Understanding who you are is the first step in living a more fulfilling life.

Your unique qualities and abilities will emerge as you pursue your life's genuine calling. While doing this, you will become more self-aware of your qualities and areas for improvement.

Embracing who you are and working to become a better version of yourself will bring excitement and assurance into your life.

✓ You will present a challenge to beliefs that are holding you back.

A strong yearning for any outcome is always the source of a person's motivation. Even if you have a clear vision of your future self, that vision may be quite different from the reality you're now experiencing.

Because of this, you can start to doubt whether or not your life's mission is really achievable, given how inadequately equipped you feel. The goal is so potent because it stretches you in constructive ways.

You'll be able to hone your abilities and discover new opportunities with its aid. The only thing you need to do to change your life is to reframe your limiting ideas. Everything in your life is a mirror of your inner state, as we discussed previously. Your next step then is to figure out why you're here.

Finding Your Life's Direction: A Step-by-Step Guide

1. Recognise and address your internal monologue.

There will be early resistance, a pervasive dread of the unknown, as you begin to delve into your thoughts and impulses.

Initially, you may have to battle your own set of assumptions. They might attempt to deter you or even persuade you that your search for meaning is madness. They may tell you demoralising things like "You don't deserve to have a purpose" or "You'll never discover what you're searching for."

You need to be aware of your internal conversation before you can stop it. Paying attention to your thoughts as they swirl reduces their intensity. They are most effective while working below the radar; therefore, bringing their activities to light will render them powerless.

2. Once you recognise these demons inside, you may begin to put an end to them.

If you wish to discover your life's meaning, the next step is to take action to alter your internal monologue.

The answer to the question "What is the point of life?" might be found in discovering your passion. This is quite simple to do. To appreciate it, you must take note of your most anticipated experiences.

Perhaps you're still searching for your life's calling. But no matter how busy you are, there's always something you wish you had more time to accomplish.

Consider the pursuits in life for which you would want to feel greater fervour. The answer to why you were sent on this earth may be found here. [5]

If you make them your everyday priorities, you will find meaning in your existence. You've reached a moment in your life when joy and contentment are overwhelming.

Helping others increases your own sense of well-being.

3. Use that golden thread to weave a picture-perfect life.

You've finally managed to tear yourself away from social media long enough to face the terrifying depths of your mind, and that means you're ready to begin the hard work of learning how to uncover and define your life's purpose. The last leg of the trip consists of piecing together the seemingly unrelated information and identifying underlying patterns.

Your current task is to examine all your responses carefully in search of shared themes between the two sets of items.

Perhaps you've always had a burning need to put pen to paper, and the act of writing each day lights you up within. Your life's mission may entail writing in some way.

Maybe you've always felt at one with nature and the great outdoors, and you've also always been captivated by the stars and the universe. This might be part of a larger outing in which you take a group of people into the wilderness to see the stars and think about their role in the cosmos.

You should let your imagination go wild while you search for your life's calling, and you shouldn't stress if you don't discover anything right away. Sometimes you just need to get some shut eye and let your mind figure everything out. Learning how to create objectives effectively is also quite useful.

If you've put in the effort, you'll soon know why you're here. When it is there, it is felt right down to the marrow of your bones.

4. Create a clear mental image of the life you want to live.

As you are clear on what matters most to you, you can begin crafting a plan to make that dream a reality.

What you tell yourself about who you are and what you tell yourself is feasible can shape how you show up each day to work towards your ultimate objective.

5. Focus on the future you want and train yourself to believe it can come true.

For instance, if you want to be a published writer, you should practice writing about subjects that interest you. Your whole set of objectives should be SMART based.

Set realistic goals and establish what you can achieve.

If you want to do something really remarkable with your life, you have to do something truly remarkable with your life. To a large extent, individuals everywhere conform their behaviour to the standards set by those around them. Their routines and timetables are based on the needs of their social networks.

Having faith in oneself is essential to pursue one's goals. If your priorities are different from those of your loved ones, this may be very difficult. Examine your priorities and identify any misleading goals you may be pursuing.

Learn Your Energy Depleters

Consider the activities that leave you feeling intellectually or physically drained. Those things need not be something you despise doing. As soon as you're able to identify these actions, you should cease taking them.

Wasteful pursuits are mentally and physically exhausting [6]. Doing so will free up your time for other important tasks, or you may delegate them entirely. Your mind, body, and heart are all sending you signals that this activity is not beneficial for you if you are becoming tired doing it.

One must run one's own race, one must live one's own life, one must pay attention to one's own priorities, and one must construct one's own vision.

Does your life have meaning to you?

Psychologists have been interested in the evolution of meaningful life goals for decades. Purpose is cultivated when one works towards a goal that has the potential to improve the lives of others, such as starting a nonprofit, discovering a cure for a deadly illness, or helping children learn to read.

Indeed, it seems that humans' sense of purpose has developed so that we might do great things together. This may be why having a sense of purpose is linked to improved physical and mental health. In an evolutionary perspective, a goal is adaptable. Both individuals and the species as a whole benefit from this.

Having a unique collection of skills and qualities is often cited as the source of finding one's life's meaning, although this is only partially true. It develops in part via interpersonal relationships, which is why feeling disconnected from others may lead to a loss of meaning in life. When you finally locate your way, you'll likely encounter people on the road who share your ultimate goal of settling down in a neighbourhood.

The following are six suggestions for overcoming loneliness and finding your life's true calling.

1.   Read.

Reading is an experience that has been connected to a greater feeling of meaning and purpose, and it links us to individuals we'll never meet across time and place. (Please take into account that "meaning" and "purpose" are distinct social scientific concepts with shared underpinnings. Meaning is a much larger term that often also encompasses value, effectiveness, and self-worth, while purpose is a subset of meaning.)

For instance, Leslie Francis discovered that among a sample of roughly 26,000 English and Welsh adolescents she researched in 2010, those who read the Bible more had a more robust sense of purpose. Reading non-religious material also appears to have an effect. Adolescents who read poetry and fiction have a greater feeling of purpose, according to a review of empirical research conducted by Raymond A. Mar and colleagues.

They speculate that "adolescents could be able to reason about the complete lives of characters in fiction, giving them precise insight into an entire lifetime without needing to have fully experienced most of their own life," through reading such works. The adage goes that if a kid can find meaning in the lives of others, they will find meaning in their own. Purpose, in this view, is a creative act.

Many of the individuals he spoke to for this piece credited books or concepts they read in books as being formative in their lives.

Art McGee, a social justice activist, was inspired by the writings of historian W. E. B. Du Bois to adopt a particular vision of African American identity and emancipation. The "social responsibility philosophy of journalism" Michael Stoll learnt about at Stanford University was a source of motivation for him as a journalist. He argued that journalists have a responsibility to help their communities by serving as "neutral arbiters of issues needing solutions." Since then, it has served as my professional compass. Motivated by this concept, Michael established the San Francisco Public Press, a nonprofit journalism organisation that has since won several awards.

So if you're having an identity crisis, go to a bookshop, library, or college. Read novels that have meaning to you, and you may get insight into what really matters in your own life.

2.   Use your pain to help others.

Obviously, the search for meaning is more than simply a mental exercise; it requires emotion. This is why it may blossom from the ashes of pain, whether our own or that of others.

Kezia Willingham grew up in a dysfunctional household with low income in Corvallis, Oregon. When she was a child, she and her brother lived in poverty and disgrace, and she was certain that her own existence was a mistake. "No one at school interfered or assisted or supported my mother, myself, or my brother," she recalled. I was taking every drug I could get my hands on, sleeping around with random people, and missing school.

Kezia attended an alternative high school when she was 16 years old and says it "gave me hope that there was a way out of poverty for me." She went to college and found herself attracted to the students with "issues" or those with problems similar to her own. Her words:

> "I hope that other kids who had a tough upbringing like mine will see that there is hope for them. I want kids to know they are brilliant, even if they fall short of the requirements set by the government. I hope kids realise their inherent worth and goodness regardless of their socioeconomic background. Just because they are. They are being bombarded with messages trying to convince them differently."

The anguish of others may sometimes illuminate our own path. High school senior Christopher Pepper was informed by a "trembling, weeping buddy" that a fellow student had sexually assaulted her. Christopher said, "I soothed as best I could and left that talk swearing that I would do something to prevent this from occurring to others." He fulfilled his word by studying to prevent rape among college students and going on to teach about sexual health in public schools in San Francisco.

As opposed to being crushed by adversity, why do certain individuals like Kezia and Christopher manage to find meaning in it? As we'll see below, one possible explanation involves the thoughts, feelings, and actions we foster inside ourselves.

3. Foster feelings of wonder, appreciation, and generosity.

Awe, gratitude, and altruism are positive feelings and actions that have been shown to improve health and well-being, and they may also help people feel like they have a purpose in life.

Feelings of wonder may serve as the "emotional basis for a sense of purpose" by strengthening our sense of connection to something greater than ourselves.

Of course, wonder isn't enough to provide meaning in and of itself. You have to be motivated to really make a difference in the world rather than simply feeling like you're a part of something bigger. That's when thanksgiving and charity come in.

It may seem contradictory to develop purpose by creating a thankful mentality, but it works. The ability to appreciate one's gifts increases one's propensity to "give to the world outside oneself." This is likely due to the fact that being made aware of the positive contributions of others increases our desire to reciprocate such gestures.

To the point now: altruism. There's no longer any doubt that a life of service to others is a life well lived. Those who volunteered more and gave more money had a stronger sense of meaning in their life.

There is a fascinating correlation between appreciation and charity and the creation of meaning and purpose. In a second study, individuals who were instructed to write letters of thanks saw an increase in their feeling of meaning in life. Acts of kindness and appreciation share neural substrates and hence stimulate similar brain reward systems.

4. Take note of the compliments you've received.

Gratitude is a path to self-discovery. However, the things for which you are most grateful may also give you a sense of meaning in life.

Many of the creative people I have encountered – painters, authors, and musicians – said that hearing positive feedback from fans and critics kept them going.

Although there is a lack of empirical evidence about the link between thankfulness and a heightened feeling of purpose, anecdotal evidence suggests that the latter may result from the former.

5. Join a group and become involved.

Consider the individuals around you if you're having problems remembering your mission. What do the two of you have in common? I don't know what they're aiming at. How do you think they will change things in the world? Is it a good thing that happened? Do you think you can help them achieve that goal by working together? Why do they need this? Is it anything you could provide to them?

If you can't find any motivation in the answers to these questions, it may be time to look for a new group of people to call home; maybe in doing so, you'll discover your life's true calling.

6. Share your experience.

Reading and writing may both aid in discovering your life's true calling.

Curiosity about one's own life may be a catalyst for finding meaning in one's own existence. What kinds of challenges have you faced? To what extent did your own strengths aid in your eventual victory? Please explain the role that other individual had in your success. When have you used your talents to make someone else's life easier?

Reasons Why a Life Without Purpose Is Unfulfilling

Each and every inspirational speaker emphasises the value of living with a mission. Everybody warns you about wandering aimlessly through life.

They are all correct. What they say is true in every way possible. Not easy, especially if you lack the internal drive to pursue your goals. It takes a lot of courage to take a random break from your life to radically alter your way of being and thinking.

Is there any greater incentive than knowing how much harm a meaningless existence is causing you?

Living without a sense of purpose may have far-reaching consequences, and these seven reasons should be more than enough to spur you on in your quest to find yours.

Having no reason to live is meaningless.

If you're like me, you sometimes fear that your life will be without meaning or purpose. If not, then you have no idea how miserable life in such a situation may be.

Try to picture yourself in a situation where you not only dread getting up every morning but also dread going to bed each night. There is no motivation to work, no enthusiasm to invest, no pleasure to be had in the company of friends, and no purpose to keep on living. A mind devoid of any thought. The inability to feel anything, either happiness or sadness. Not looking forward to anything.

It's obvious that living in such society is rather miserable. That's how it feels when you don't have anything to live for.

An aimless existence leads to no accomplishments. Nothing is guiding you towards some made-up goal. You are in a hopeless situation in which you are unable to reach your destination, are suffering immensely while traveling there, and despise the path you must take to get there.

If you do have any kind of plans at all, they are quite unstructured. These two aims are incompatible. It's clear you have no idea where you're going. The futility of a life without a purpose.

The wider picture becomes clearer though if you have a firm grasp on your life's ultimate purpose. Each and every one of these actions matters. There is a purpose to your travels, and they are not aimless. Instead, you may take pleasure in the walks themselves since you know they are ultimately getting you to your destination.

It's No Wonder You're Nervous

Do you feel that your life is a constant source of worry? It's probably because you don't have something worthwhile to work for.

There is no use in living if you don't have something to live for. There is no correlation between any of your actions. Nothing makes sense; therefore, your brain has trouble making sense of what's going on.

Anxiety develops when a person's rational thinking concludes that they are in imminent risk of losing their lives. Without meaning in life, your brain interprets isolation as a potential danger to survival. Your brain has been trained to see everything that doesn't belong as potentially harmful.

In contrast, things make more sense if you give your actions a greater meaning. As a result, you're experiencing less stress and worry. Your worries have subsided since you realise the journey itself isn't futile.

Inspiration Is a Lost Hope

High levels of motivation are a must for every human being serious about achieving their goals.

If you want to see things more plainly, try doing so from the premise that your life has a specific goal. It's as though you blindly follow wherever life takes you. I don't even know what that does.

It's a mental energy booster. There's a sense of growing anticipation as you make progress towards your goal. Because of this, you'll be motivated to improve immediately.

Without a driving motivation, it's impossible to reach the highest levels of success. Your lack of insight into its ultimate destination has led you to dismiss it as unimportant. But even the tiniest gain is a motivation booster when you know exactly what you're working for.

Finding and adhering to one's life's purpose is the single most effective way to maintain motivation.

Distraction Prevents Development

Every discipline, occupation, aspect of life, and relationship has room for improvement. The name of progress is human life; even if your physical abilities don't improve, your mind will.

Can we trace the origins of this expansion? The greatest informational resources could be made available to you. However, you won't pick up a single letter unless your brain is in the right place to do so. It's the same with life; even the most seemingly meaningless incidents may teach you something if you pay attention.

The way it works is that having a goal in life keeps you focused. The final result is predictable, albeit you may take a few detours along the way. So in the grand scheme of things, all your efforts are serving a greater purpose.

Without this single-mindedness, success is impossible. If you have something you're working towards, it will inform your decisions about everything, from your job to your social circle to your apartment to your daily commute. You may carry your undivided attention with you everywhere you go. The intended result is constant throughout.

If you keep your mind on the correct things, you won't even notice the little things that are bothering you. No matter how little anything may seem, you should keep your attention on what really matters. Having a clear goal in life makes it much simpler to exert one's best effort in all endeavours.

It's Hard to Seemingly Achieve Anything When Your Life Seems Pointless

Everything you've read so far has a direct bearing on whether or not you succeed. To be successful in any endeavour, therefore, it is crucial to cultivate inner calm, intrinsic drive, and laser-like concentration. However, these just scratch the surface.

If you don't know what you're here for in this world, you may still have a vision. To keep moving in what you believe to be the correct way, you may even force yourself to your absolute limits.

Consider this alternative:

> You want to go to New York but find yourself in the incorrect place entirely. It's dark, and the road is narrow when you first set foot on it, but you go on. Your automobile malfunctions, and there is no repair shop in the area to take it in. But you drive the vehicle as far as it will go. Keep going forever, and you won't get to New York.

> Therefore, no amount of effort will be fruitful if you don't know your life's purpose. In other words, you may only need to put in half the effort if you know you're on the correct track.

It Has a Negative Impact on Physical Health

Living a meaningless existence has negative consequences for more than just the mind. It might also have a toll on your physical health.

You will first notice a physical manifestation of the mental stress. Hair loss, acne, weight loss, weight gain, and other health problems may all be brought on by chronic stress. There may also be more dire results.

Scientific research has shown that persons who have defined goals in life tend to outlive those who don't. People who knew what they were living for had a higher pain threshold and lower risk of cardiovascular disease.

Furthermore, striking is the fact that those who lack meaning in life are 2.4 times more likely to get Alzheimer's disease.

One possible explanation is that those who feel their lives have no meaning also lack optimism and anticipation. They are affected physically because of how they feel mentally. If having a clear goal in life may help you avoid these problems, then why not pursue one?

There Is No Pleasure in Life

Being accepted by one's peers is crucial to fulfilling one's potential. Those who have no goals in life are more likely to feel alone. Their enjoyment of social events decreases even if they participate.

Because of their lack of mental clarity, such persons are unable to take pleasure in the world around them. As a result of neurological deficiencies, they are unable to understand feelings. However, this does not always imply that their current situation is unacceptable. If you're in a positive mental state, you may find that you love spending time with the same people and in the same setting.

Each explanation can be traced back to having no clear direction in life, and each cause contributes to a life of chaos. No one would knowingly want to be subjected to that kind of existence.

We've only got a small amount of time to enjoy this planet. So stop squandering it on meaninglessness and start working to better your life.

You have the power to free yourself from this painful existence. Put up with the trouble and temporary difficulty to have a life worth living for all of eternity!

CHAPTER ——————— 10

Maintain Confidence in Your Capabilities

People who are secure in their own abilities are certain that they can overcome whatever obstacle they face. Confident and upbeat, they are not afraid to take risks or work towards their objectives, no matter how daunting they may first seem.

Having self-assurance in the workplace is important for many reasons. Having confidence in oneself may make one less worried and agitated while simultaneously increasing drive and ambition. Although some people seem to be born with an innate sense of confidence, most of us have to work at it.

Here are ten suggestions to help you feel better about yourself and bring that confidence to the job.

Tips for Boosting Your Confidence at Work

The following methods will help you gain self-assurance in the job while improving your professional growth and abilities:

- ### Engage in continuing education for your career

Investing in yourself to hone the abilities you need to succeed at work can boost your confidence in other areas of your life. Improving one's performance in one's job may be attributed in part to one's increased self-assurance, which in turn can be attributed to one's increased mastery of that skill.

Think about enrolling in a course to hone your talents or further your career. You may increase your credentials by, perhaps, taking a course in project management or going to a training seminar or reading relevant periodicals and books.

- ## Acquire fresh abilities

In the same way that honing your existing abilities may boost your self-assurance, so can expanding your knowledge base and advancing your education. Putting your learning to the test is a great way to gauge both your progress and your dedication to furthering your education, both of which may assist in enhancing your self-assurance. A person's productivity and capacity to maintain order and comfort with taking on new challenges at work may all benefit from the acquisition of new knowledge and the subsequent use of that knowledge.

If you want to go forward in your career, here's how to improve your skill set.

- ## Dress to impress

Think about what you'd wear if you were applying for an important project or job in a corporate setting and try to make those clothes more appropriate for that setting. If you have a business casual dress code, for instance, you may wear casual slacks instead of jeans.

You may find that your level of self-assurance in carrying out your duties and communicating with your clients/co-workers and superiors increases if you try to dress and present yourself more professionally for work. Wearing jeans to a business meeting is as inappropriate as wearing flip-flops to a wedding.

Taking a risk is a difficult confidence-building tactic to implement, but it may pay off in the long run. Perhaps you have always dreaded presenting in front of the entire marketing and sales department. You can force yourself out of your comfort zone by offering to give the next presentation or co-host with a colleague. It is at this point that you would start working on your presentation.

You'd have to push yourself to the limits, but keeping your mind on the positives – your abilities, your plan for delivering the presentation, and the content itself – instead of the potential pitfalls and potential embarrassment can help you overcome your anxiety and feel more secure in your professional abilities.

Leaving your safe space can also help you spot opportunities you would have overlooked otherwise. If you avoid stepping out of your comfort zone and giving the presentation, you might be missing out on an opportunity to make an important career move or gain valuable new clients.

See this for a related article on enhancing your oratory abilities in front of an audience:

- ## Model your behaviour after more assured friends

Think about the people you know who have achieved success or find someone who seems competent and at ease in their position and study their behaviour. You can boost your own self-assurance by adopting some practices you see self-assured friends and colleagues are using in their careers.

- ## Set goals

Making both short-term and long-term plans for your career can change how you feel about your abilities and accomplishments. Think about establishing a target for yourself to increase your general competence or acquire a brand-new skill. Evaluate your progress even further by setting manageable intermediate goals. Keeping track of your progress and celebrating even the smallest victories along the way can do wonders for your self-assurance, as you will be able to see exactly where your efforts are paying off and how you are growing as a result.

If you want to improve your work life, one goal you could set is to work harder. After deciding on a long-term objective, you can break it down into more manageable sub-goals, such as learning to prioritise your work or completing one task at a time. Achieving small wins on the path to greater productivity can boost your self-assurance and allow you to do better work.

- **Play to your strengths**

Taking stock of your accomplishments and skillsets is an integral part of identifying and focusing on your strengths, which can in turn boost your self-assurance. Professionals who strive for perfection often lose sight of the big picture in favour of picking apart every last detail of their work.

If this describes you, you might find it helpful to write down your skills and strengths, followed by a list of your accomplishments. Read them first thing in the morning and whenever you need a pick-me-up throughout the day.

- **Gain wisdom from past errors**

Implementing improvement plans and goal-setting strategies inevitably involves making some blunders. The secret is to take a hard look at your blunders and figure out how you can prevent them in the future. Recognising and accepting defeat is challenging, but it can shape how you approach future challenges.

For instance, if you accidentally entered the wrong code into a data entry program, rather than retyping everything from scratch, you could look at the spot where you made the error and determine whether it was the result of carelessness or a truly flawed piece of information. If you take the time to reflect on your actions and identify what went wrong, you'll be better equipped to avoid making the same mistake again.

• Remove all pessimistic language

Taking stock of your own self-perception is another important step in boosting your self-assurance. Take action if you realise you are overly critical of yourself or give yourself frequent opportunities to doubt your abilities. Self-affirming methods may include writing down your top professional talents or reflecting on all the good things that have happened to you in the last week.

Keep track of your professional growth and give yourself credit when you finish a project well or go above and beyond what was asked of you.

Taking an active role in your own education and not being afraid to ask questions can do wonders for your professional self-assurance. Start making it a habit to ask at least one question during team meetings, project planning sessions, and conferences if there's information that's unclear to you.

Doing so as a regular part of your work routine can increase your feelings of confidence and self-worth through contribution, and it can also show your team members and supervisors that you will take initiative when you feel you might need more direction. Your willingness to speak up and ask questions can be an inspiration to your co-workers who may be struggling with their own self-assurance.

You should take things slowly and patiently as you work to improve your career. You should create a schedule with reasonable deadlines for accomplishing your goals, and you should also think about using a checklist or spreadsheet to keep tabs on your progress.

Keeping at it: It takes time to make a change, so you may need to readjust your plans accordingly. The only way to guarantee that you keep making progress towards boosting your self-assurance is to remain consistent in your actions and improvement plans.

Keep expanding your way of thinking: Self-reflection and self-evaluation can be more fruitful if you approach them with a growth mindset. Boosting your self-assurance at work can be as simple as welcoming challenges, triumphing over setbacks, and celebrating your achievements.

CHAPTER ——————— 11

Reflect and Move On

E very day, you make an effort to survive and advance towards your objectives.

It might be discouraging to feel like you're making no progress at all.

Do you ever think about giving introspection a try? Or maybe you're wondering what it is you should think about.

Thinking back on one's accomplishments, good or poor, is an act of self-reflection.

It's a great tool for taking stock of your progress and identifying areas for improvement.

The Meaning of Introspection

Self-reflection entails inspecting and critiquing several facets of one's existence. That is to say this may also be a metaphor for contemplation or looking inside.

Self-reflection is a lot like explaining what you see when you look in the mirror, except that it may occasionally reveal aspects of yourself that are hidden from view.

It's important to check in with ourselves now and again to see whether we're actually happy and pleased with our life and, if not, to remember that we always have the power to make some changes.

Many individuals dislike introspection because it forces them to confront both their strengths and their flaws.

The path to become the finest possible version of oneself requires regular introspection.

Doing so requires keeping yourself accountable for the choices and activities you've determined are essential to your development, despite the fact that we're always evolving.

Achieving your full potential is impossible if you refuse to examine your own actions and thoughts. It'll help you figure out what's going on inside your head and heart and why you're feeling the way you are.

For context, when you take the time to focus on yourself, you may learn more about your identity and the factors that shape it.

The task of sorting through your emotions and ideas might be simplified if you can identify and understand their origins. Self-reflection is, to some extent, synonymous with self-awareness.

Consideration of Oneself

At the end of the day, month, or year, we may all benefit from a moment of reflection on our behaviour to learn from our mistakes and improve for the future.

Spending time figuring out what needs our attention provides us with a map for the road ahead.

Many individuals merely walk-through life without giving any thought to their actions.

There's no better way to set yourself up for failure and poor habits. These folks can be unknowingly spreading negativity.

These unfortunate events may be a direct result of their own choices, which leaves people baffled.

On the other hand, you may be reaping the benefits of doing something properly without ever knowing what it was that you did right.

Self-reflection is a useful tool for assessing and improving one's performance in life.

The Positive Effects of Introspection

There are a number of positive outcomes that may result from taking the time to examine your own actions and accomplishments.

1. Stronger Connections

Self-reflection is useful when dealing with a new relationship or even a quarrel.

You don't have to make a hasty choice based on how you feel in the moment about the connection. Instead, you may take some time to reflect on your feelings and the issue at hand.

Relationships with romantic partners, toxic friends, or family members or even just getting to know someone new may all benefit from this.

2. Gained Confidence in One's Own Identity

Many individuals seldom get the opportunity to sit quietly with themselves, and this is exactly what you'll do when you engage in self-reflection or introspection.

It's necessary for development, although it may be quite unpleasant at times.

When you have some time to think, you may tune out the world and focus on yourself.

How do you feel physically and emotionally? How are you doing medically? What are you most interested in?

When you have a deep understanding of who you are, you can face the challenges of life with confidence and serenity.

3. Ability to Make Sound Choices

In addition to improving one's understanding of oneself via introspection, one also has the benefit of enhanced decision-making clarity.

You shouldn't second-guess yourself while making a choice if you have a solid grasp of who you are and what you value.

It ought to be obvious to you what to do. There will be a lot less wondering and tension for you as a result of this.

Methods of Reflection: 15 Techniques

1.   Identify key issues

Prepare an evaluation of your self-reflection by thinking of questions you'll want to ask yourself on a regular basis (daily, weekly, monthly).

To provide a few instances:

Where do my new behaviours stand after this last week?
In what ways can I advance?
Where do I stand with how I felt today?

2.   Think deeply and reflectively

There's no need to worry about being great at this; in fact, the discomfort is part of the learning process.

But try to go as long as you can without speaking and see where your thoughts take you.

Exactly what are your mental processes?

Recognise it and give some attention to the air you're taking in and letting out.

3.   Write a journal

Keeping a diary or journal is a terrific method to express yourself in writing.

It's a handy record to have so you may analyse your behaviour and mental patterns afterwards.

4. Do some kind of writing practice

Do you find that your ideas and choices keep getting mixed up in your head?

Get out a timer and use the next five to ten minutes to write anything that comes to mind.

Found any repeating themes? What kinds of ideas should you hold onto, and what kinds should you let go?

Doing writing exercises is a terrific way to get your ideas down on paper (or screen) and get your thoughts in order. You are free to think about them anytime you choose.

5. Go for a hike in the woods

Taking a walk in the fresh air has been proved to boost morale. Take a walk outside and regain your composure.

When engaging in introspective thinking, it's ideal to do it in a serene and conducive setting.

6. Have an internal dialogue

A fantastic approach to get epiphanies is to listen to oneself speak aloud.

Conversation with oneself is a great way to release pent-up emotions and gain insight about oneself.

7. Do some breathing exercises

Breathing exercises, whether they are basic or sophisticated, may help you maintain a constant heart rate and reduce stress. They help you relax so that you can think more clearly.

8.   Read self-help books

Reading nonfiction has given me some of my most profound moments of self-realisation. You learn to identify your own preferences for activities and foods.

Reading is the ultimate meditative practice.

9.   Take a look back at something that happened in the past

Select a time period that has strong emotions for you. Ponder it for a while.

Explain your reaction to the occurrence.

Explain what it was that you achieved well in this specific competition. Where do you see room for development in the future?

10. Reflect on what you have to be thankful for

Whenever you wind down for the day, take a moment to reflect on the three things for which you are most thankful. Spend some time thinking about them by yourself.

11. Sign up for a yoga session

The advantages of doing yoga in a serene setting are many.

The possibilities for improvement in flexibility and respiratory health are two such outcomes.

You may use this time to reflect, meditate, or think things over. This is an excellent opportunity for introspection.

12. Measure how you're feeling

Do yourself a favour and keep a notebook or use a mobile app to record your daily emotions.

Are there any patterns to how you're feeling?

Understanding your reaction to a given prejudice might provide you calm and an understanding of your actions.

It's time for you to do a self-check, which is step number 1.

13. Take some time alone

Just take some time alone and take stock of your situation.

Life goals include things such as professional development, romantic relationships, academic success, extracurricular involvement, family stability, physical health, and fitness.

What is your level of satisfaction with how you've performed in each category? In what ways might you begin to enhance your performance?

14. Establish detailed objectives

After you engage in the aforementioned acts of self-reflection, creating concrete objectives to reach may boost your performance considerably.

In what state do you want to find yourself emotionally and physically in the following half year? Three years? Five years?

Seeing yourself succeeding at these endeavours is a powerful motivator.

I suggest MasterClass, a customisable program with a variety of lessons on many subjects, if you're having trouble determining what to set as your objectives.

15. Attempt talk therapy

Counselling or therapy with a trained expert may provide a safe space for you to discuss personal issues without fear of criticism.

Your counsellor will encourage you to go deeply inside yourself and discover new insights.

Online therapy appeals to me because of the convenience and adaptability it provides.

Some Reflective Examples

Here are some real-world examples of how to put the above advice into reality via self-reflection:

Get outside once a week for at least thirty minutes.

Just pay attention to what you're experiencing emotionally and mentally.

Get some more sleep in. Grab a cup of coffee and curl up with a book you're looking forward to reading.

Spend five minutes a day alone in a dark room thinking about anything you choose. It's best to try to put more time on as you go.

These days have been a little stressful for you. It seems as if your thoughts are all over the place. Put five minutes on the clock and jot down everything you can think of.

You will feel overwhelmed, but after seeing your to-do list and your thoughts, you will calm down.

Focus on analysing a recurring dream concerning a former occurrence. You will learn what about that experience was so stressful for you.

Consider a routine you regularly engage in. You will gain self-awareness and may begin instantly bettering yourself by changing this behaviour.

What Role Does Self-Reflection Play in Personal Development?

When you make time for introspection, you get perspective on your whole existence.

You know yourself inside and out, and as a result, you are never startled by your emotions or actions.

As discussed before, this helps you improve in every aspect. Stop trying to escape who you are and start making the most of who you are.

When you know who you are at your core, no one can use that against you.

As a result, you feel more at ease and confident in your own skin. Fear and insecurity stem in large part from the unwillingness to accept our own humanity and its inherent frailties.

There is no cause for insecurity if you have done the introspective work required to realise who you are.

Realising that you can improve yourself in any manner, whether by focusing on your flaws or your strengths, is a powerful step towards being a better person.

For instance, if your flaw is the inability to deal with irritation, you might practice relaxing about things you can't change and concentrating on those you can.

These are the kind of insights that come from practicing regular introspection.

If you allow your feelings to take over, you could go crazy. But if you figure out what's really behind them, you'll find it much simpler to accept and let go of them.

Because of this, it's clear that introspection is a powerful tool for personal growth.

Having a stronger sense of identity may be achieved through daily introspection.

Having a stronger sense of identity can help you in many aspects of your daily life, including your interactions with others and the choices you make.

C HAPTER ——————— 12

Things to Do When You Have No Motivation to Do Anything

Y ou are probably feeling tight and confined because of the constant barrage of requests and alerts that you get when you are reading this book. The last thing you want when you don't feel like doing anything is to read a bunch of confusing information that makes your brain hurt.

To help you deal with this issue effectively, I'll provide you with some suggestions that will help you get back on track.

It's normal to feel this way sometimes. Even the most senior, influential, and well-known among us might feel demoralised by the increased global uncertainty we're presently experiencing.

The trick is to detect the indicators of the loss of motivation and act quickly on the fifteen actionable suggestions that follow so that you may once again embrace your full potential, reconnect with your larger vision, and feel the spark of joy within that feeds your motivation.

Tips to Get Moving When You Feel Like Doing Nothing

If you are feeling demotivated, try these fifteen strategies:

1. Get rid of your critical mind first.

Once you realise you have zero drive to change your situation, the first step is to forgive yourself. If you're not as physically active or driven as you'd want to be, try not to be too hard on yourself.

The tiredness, mental fatigue, and lethargy that we are attempting to avoid may be exacerbated when ambitious people judge themselves negatively for not living up to an ideal.

If this describes you, I urge you to pause for a moment and commit to being more deliberate in your approach and less harsh on yourself for wanting to take a break and recharge.

2. Keep in mind the motivation behind your action.

Consider your reasons for wanting to write the post if you find yourself feeling uninspired. The motivations you have for doing something are what ultimately cause you to act. Only when your motivation is both compelling and personal will you go to any lengths to achieve your goal.

When you have zero interest in doing anything, it's because the reason for doing it isn't compelling enough. A simple definition of motivation is the mental and emotional state that prompts and sustains action in pursuit of a desired outcome. The question to ponder is why individuals decide to give up smoking. The majority of smokers give up the habit because they fear for their health or the health of their loved ones if they don't.

What motivates you to act in this way? Is there a particular reason you wish to reach your objectives? Try to provide convincing, heartfelt explanations. If you're struggling to get started on a task, remind yourself of why you want to complete it.

3.   Rethink its significance.

Revise your notion of self-care to include putting your own renewal first. To be honest, I find this a little unsettling at times.

I used to struggle with being alone with my thoughts, but I've learned to appreciate the peace and quiet of solitude and even welcome it.

To do this, you must change your perspective and see rejuvenation as an act of forward movement and constructive action. In this approach, you should allow the process of rebuilding take its natural course rather than always looking for new ways to gain ground.

Allow yourself some time to refocus and take charge of your own refuelling. At some point, every top performer makes this link, and once they do, they never look back.

4.   Think about the pros and cons without exclusion.

There is no cost for using visualisation, but it is a very powerful tool at our disposal. You are free to entertain any thought or idea at any time and in any place.

Here's a workout to try:

Let's pretend you're in the kitchen and you see a bright large lemon in the fridge. The next step is to grab a knife and divide the lemon into two.

Speculate about this in great depth and detail. Now that you've sliced the lemon in half, pick up the half, and squeeze it so that the juice runs into your mouth. Imagine the squeezing action, complete with the sound it creates, and the tangy taste of fresh lemon juice in your lips. Is there more saliva in your mouth now or none at all?

The quantity of saliva in your mouth is likely to increase if you imagine this process in great detail. Your brain has trouble telling the difference between reality and fantasy, and this is the result.

Because of this, visualising data is an effective technique. If you've always wanted to own a Mercedes Benz, try to conjure up a mental image of yourself doing so. Visualise the exact make and model you're after, along with its colour, interior scent, how the steering wheel would feel, and the sound of the engine revving. Do you believe that one day your thoughts will manifest into reality?

The idea is that mental imagery can boost your motivation and help you achieve your goals. Imagining yourself in the automobile of your dreams can spark a fire of intrinsic drive. When you feel unmotivated and feel like procrastinating, do this.

The more you can get yourself to imagine a future in which you have already achieved your goals and put yourself in that state of mind on a consistent basis, the more likely it is that you will really achieve those goals.

Focusing on anything strengthens it. Thus, it's important to be mindful of the ideas and beliefs you hold dear.

5. Acknowledge your feelings.

When you give yourself permission to feel what you feel, you put some distance between yourself and your emotional response. If you're feeling unmotivated right now, here is the place to pick yourself up and decide how you want to present yourself to the world and to yourself.

A pause occurs between the stimulus and the reaction. Right there where we can decide how to react is our agency. The nicest part is knowing ahead of time that you won't be very patient with foolishness, roadblocks, or little annoyances since you won't be motivated to overcome them.

They may be anything, from a lost taxi driver to an unpleasant customer service representative to a complicated payment system or an incomprehensible procedure. Let me tell you, if you don't learn to control your feelings and show yourself some self-love, it'll drive you crazy.

This is the way to go, but it requires practice.

When you feel like doing nothing, it's a sign that your energy is low, and you need to take immediate steps to restore it across the board – in your mind, body, emotions, and spirit.

6. Reduce complexity.

If you're an optimist, you'll think it's wonderful. To you, development is second nature, and the larger picture is what drives you. You end up saying yes to everything because you don't have time to think about how you really feel about the commitments you've made.

Your life becomes a never-ending stream of events, and as with any repetitive task, it may lead to boredom, a lack of inspiration, and eventually burnout.

There's no surprise that we feel a bit ragged around the edges if we don't take the time to recover from this state of high alert and continual responsiveness we're forced to maintain on a daily basis.

This implies that finding a solution to a problem requires stepping back from the urgency of daily living, turning off unnecessary distractions, and simplifying the situation.

Your vitality is being eroded by your increasing list of obligations. The energy you possess is priceless; protect it as such.

Reducing your obligations by half is the quickest approach to boost your performance. According to James Clear's book *Atomic Habits*, taking a break allows you to refocus on the here and now, prioritise your own needs, and get yourself back on track.

Getting rid of social "musts," unnecessary Zoom calls, and nagging alerts frees up time and space for you to focus on the next stages in the process of discovering your passion.

There's more than one use for airplane mode! Do not neglect its usage.

7. Go to bed, you sleepyhead.

When we are very drained, we find it difficult to tap into our creative genius, and our zest for life dulls or even disappears for a while.

Now is the time to make getting enough good sleep a top priority. Learning to tune in to your body and make necessary adjustments helps speed up the process. Try to make it a habit to turn in by 9:30 every night.

Inadequate sleep has been linked to a wide range of unfavourable health outcomes, including cardiovascular disease, a compromised immune system, diabetes type 2, and mental health issues, including anxiety and despair.

It is tempting to read emails at work just before bed, but you should refrain from doing it. Even better, switch your phone to airplane mode so you won't be disturbed at all.

8. Recognise yourself as a learner and honour that quality.

What you use to evaluate yourself is significant.

If you've built your sense of worth on being a high achiever, your sales numbers, or your knowledge, your confidence will plummet if your performance drops.

You won't get happiness and prosperity by following this plan.

Tom Bilyeu, co-founder of Impact Theory, advocates for respecting oneself and keeping a "white belt" mindset because of the antifragility of learning. *Antifragile* refers to the property of an object or system to get stronger under stress as opposed to breaking at its ultimate limit.

When compared with resilience and robustness, antifragility is a whole different concept. The resilient can shrug off change and keep functioning normally, whereas the antifragile actually improves with time.

9.   Stay away from bad company.

You probably already know that your disposition is influenced by your immediate environment, but did you realise that your surroundings may also have an effect?

When you spend enough time with a group of individuals, you start to take on their traits. The more time you spend in the company of successful individuals who are continuously discussing how they are developing and expanding their knowledge, the more likely you are to do the same. To combat a lack of drive, try changing your surroundings to ones that naturally inspire you.

However, if you spend your time with individuals who are always complaining about others, you will feel down and unmotivated yourself. A negative work atmosphere may be to blame.

If you want to feel motivated to go to work each day, it's important to create a pleasant and encouraging office. Keep in mind that the setting in which you find yourself is significant and might have an effect on your state of mind. Don't allow your circumstances to control you. Instead, take action to alter them. Right now, it's vital that you put some distance between yourself and those who are a drain on your energies.

Determination decreases when we feel like doing nothing, and this affects our ability to make good choices. You'll bring down your mood if you spend time with gloomy, negative complainers. Getting in touch with one's inner self is the key to emerging from the shadows and into the light.

10. Adapt your body and keep moving.

The act of moving itself evokes feelings. If you're feeling sad and unmotivated, try altering your physiological state.

If you're looking for a first exercise to try, here it is:

Make an effort to feel down by recalling terrible experiences and seeing how your body reacts. Watch your breathing, posture, and face. Specifically, where are your hands, and are you looking up or down?

Your motivation decreases in the short term as your body reacts physiologically to your emotional state of sadness. On the other hand, if you're in a good mood and full of pep, your body will show it. Most people's respiration rates, hand gestures, speech rates, and gaze directions all speed up and become more forward focused when they are feeling enthusiastic and inspired.

This is why it is usually rather simple to deduce whether a person is sad or joyful based only on their body language. Changing your physical condition may have a profound effect on your mental and emotional well-being.

You may lessen your worrying and overthinking by starting a forward momentum by acting on the things you can control. To avoid experiencing feelings of being overwhelmed, this must be done carefully.

Give this a shot:

Get started by making a list of your objectives and the knowledge gaps you need to fill to achieve them. This is what I mean when I talk about making "proactive progress."

Instead of sitting around and hoping for things to happen, you should go out and make it happen.

In the next step, you need to dissect each aim into its simplest components.

Since your strength is already low, it is important that we minimise mental exertion so you don't have to use any more of it trying to remember what to do next. Here's how: Maintain a list in your phone's notes of the three things you care most about completing.

When your stamina and patience are at an all-time low, this will help you maintain concentration.

In this state of low vitality, you'll benefit greatly from a system or instrument that serves to promptly provide you with directions and other pertinent information. This is significant since crossing accomplishments off your list, no matter how minor, is a great confidence booster.

11. Think about the chances, not the odds.

When we're completely depleted and unable to go another mile, it's no wonder our drive dries up. When you don't put the correct things into your body, it's tough to feel energised and full of life.

Taking the day off, ignoring your inbox, and relaxing in front of the TV while snacking on your favourite food is all part of it. Nothing wrong with it at all.

This also provides a little opening through which you may allow your thoughts to return to a place of open possibilities, roam, and dream. This, in turn, allows you to re-establish contact with your overarching goals and get insight into the areas where you've been misplacing your focus.

When we're in the middle of things, it's easy to forget about our own needs in favour of those of others around us. The flame inside may be reignited by taking a step back and concentrating on one's own development, thoughts, potential, and purpose.

The goal, as put out by author Idil Ahmed, is to become aware of our inner glance. From Ahmed's definition, a glimpse into one's own mind entails the following:

> At "the precise time" when "a spiritual epiphany reminds you of your potential, your strength, and the capacity to envision in your imagination the variety of possibilities within your reach," you will have arrived.

12. Donate to charity.

One of the simplest methods to get back in sync with our larger vision when we are feeling out of sync with the world and lack drive is to assist another person. One way to do this is to assist a buddy in preparing for a job interview or just listen to them speak about their own experiences.

Giving is not limited to monetary donations. As easy as it may seem, all it takes is to make someone happy or give them a sense of agency to change someone's day.

13. Be careful with your words.

If you want to go from slouching on the couch, hardly able to muster the mental energy necessary to determine which program to watch on Netflix, to a bubbling puddle of excitement and drive, pay attention to the words you use to motivate yourself.

Listen carefully to what you're saying to yourself and out loud. Instead of pessimism, self-pity, and despair, they should convey positivism, solutions, optimism, and passion.

You're fighting a battle that can only be won by defeating yourself. Improve your chances of reaching your goals by learning from your mistakes and gradually increasing the bar for what you'll allow in your daily life.

14. Be inspired by those around you.

When you're feeling demotivated, it might be helpful to read a motivational book, listen to motivational music, or watch an inspirational film. Start your day off well by devoting at least thirty minutes to reading motivational material. This will help you get your day off to a positive start and carry you through any difficulties you may encounter.

Inspiration may also be found in the form of videos and music. When you're feeling depressed and unmotivated, try listening to a motivating podcast or viewing an inspirational video on YouTube. You'll be energised and prepared to go in no time.

15. Stop for rest when you need it.

If you're feeling uninspired, it's okay to take a break. Keep in mind that achievement is not a final goal but rather a process that takes time and effort. People often wrongly believe that if they only do one remarkable thing, they will instantly become successful.

However, it's the ability to keep going the distance that separates those who succeed from those who fail. They are always doing something, and they never give up. The road to lasting success is long and arduous.

Take breaks when you need to and get adequate sleep. Realise what you're capable of and what you may reasonably expect of yourself. If you've been productive, you deserve some downtime. After a good night's sleep, you'll feel refreshed and ready to take on the world again.

Inspired Again: The Secret of Steve Jobs's Success

Steve Jobs, speaking at Stanford University's graduation ceremony, joked that delivering his commencement address to the students was as near as he'd ever get to receiving his own diploma. He never completed his degree. His education expenses were paid for by the life savings his parents had accumulated as working-class people. He tried it for six months but ultimately decided it wasn't worth the time and effort. He was at a crossroads in his life and chose to enrol in a calligraphy course as an escape. But he couldn't think of a single situation in which that collection of abilities would be useful.

Jobs took a calligraphy class in the 1970s, and by the 1980s, he was using the knowledge he gained there to build the Macintosh computer.

When you're trying to go somewhere, sometimes you can't see how to get there from where you are. Even if you don't have a clear idea of where you're heading or a mapped-out plan, you have to have confidence in yourself and know that you will succeed in achieving your goals. No one can see the whole picture going forward, but looking back, everything starts to make sense.

Tim Ferriss: Letting Circumstances Set Your Mood

The notion of taking use of one's surroundings is one that Tim Ferriss, creator of the *4-Hour Workweek*, has long championed. He thinks it's more beneficial to exercise control over one's surroundings than to depend on just self-discipline. Midnight until three or four in the morning are his most productive writing hours. He likes to pretend he's in a social setting while writing by watching a movie with the sound muted and a cup of tea in his hand.

Take a quick look at the area immediately around you. What kind of feelings does it evoke in you? How much inspiration does it provide? Is it noisy or quiet? Forcing ourselves to work while our minds are telling us otherwise is one of life's most taxing experiences.

You will feel worse and be less productive if you are always attempting to discipline yourself. As an alternative, focus on creating your ideal working environment and schedule. Remove all the noise and clutter. If you find that you are at your most productive and energised in the wee hours of the night, try starting your workday at midnight. Realising the importance of a conducive work setting may boost your mood and make you more productive.

How to Get Rid of Negative Thoughts and Change Your Thinking Pattern

I t's common to struggle with pessimism, and that weight might seem heavy at times. That's why it's natural to want to know how to stop thinking negatively all the time. You may be surprised to learn that the solution to this puzzle is easier to understand than you think.

The noise and steady flow of negative ideas, even if they are warranted, may make even the smallest things seem insignificant. What would you do if you could just tune out that roar?

Try something new, like a different major or a different line of work. It's not that you're always dwelling on pessimistic, self-defeating ideas.

The thought that we could say something bad is always at the back of our minds. Here are several approaches to learning why negative thoughts are so perilous and how to counteract them.

How to Stop Thinking Negative Thoughts

Learn some tried-and-true methods for letting destructive ideas go where they belong.

• Recognise the causes

Look for patterns in these spirals as you learn to watch your thoughts dispassionately. What usually sets off this downward spiral if anything? Not content with that realisation? Keep going.

Investigate more to learn what causes these reactions and what feelings are driving them. Why do you think the trigger is having such an effect on you? Any lingering problems down there? Try to get to the bottom of the problem rather than just treating the symptoms.

Consult a therapist if you need help processing the emotions involved. In the long term, these spirals may be broken if the underlying wounds or damaged scars are healed.

• Read aloud

These days it's all the rage for celebrities to read their most hateful social media comments aloud, and the effect is hilarious in its absurdity. Give that critical thought in your brain a try. Talk it out with a buddy who will help you see the humour in your mind's absurdity.

Saying them aloud will alter the atmosphere surrounding the concept, making it simpler to let go and replace it with a more positive one. This one piece of advice on how to cope with negative thoughts can change your life in ways you never imagined.

• Recount a humorous anecdote

A good mood may be maintained forever after a good laugh. Try to lighten the mood with a grin, a joke, or a humorous memory. One of life's greatest benefits is the ability to laugh at oneself. The joy and health that come from finding something to laugh at every day are two of the many ways in which laughter enriches one's life.

Keep in mind that you may always use this strategy to fight off any unfavourable ideas that may enter your mind. You don't have to crack jokes about absolutely everything, however. That doing something humorous might help you overcome gloomy thoughts is a simple yet powerful idea.

• Respond

Negative ideas, like being in power, are a burden. Whenever they attempt to take over, just imitate what I do. Send a silent "thank you for sharing" to it in your mind and go on with your day. Trying to silence it will just make it louder, so don't bother. If anything negative is said to you, just answer it and go on.

It takes effort to stick to this advice. If you find yourself thinking negatively, stop yourself. That you are aware of it means you can respond and redirect the thinking to something else. Put on that outfit, and if you're having a terrible self-esteem moment, take a deep breath and check out your reflection in the mirror. Remind yourself that you are capable and attractive rather than putting yourself down.

• Take a deep breath

Take three long breaths to relax your mind. Put an end to what you're doing, plant your feet firmly on the ground, and take a few deep breaths. Don't panic. Take a deep breath and figure out what to do next.

Meditation begins with a simple breath. Therefore, it is a crucial aspect of the meditation process. Feel the air entering your nose and traveling down your throat as you take deep breaths in and out. Silently counting your inhalations and exhalations is another kind of breath-based meditation that may help divert your attention from racing thoughts.

As with any kind of meditation, all it takes is a little mindfulness to benefit from focusing on one's breathing. Try this suggestion and see whether it helps you unwind.

• Set a deadline

Spending time with depressing ideas won't make them disappear. Try telling yourself that you'll give those ideas a minute of your time and then they'll be kicked to the curb. Set a timer on your phone to give yourself a little more push. Avoid thinking negatively once the alarm has sounded.

This practical advice for overcoming pessimism is simple enough for novices to use right now. When a bad notion first enters your mind, you can't just force yourself to ignore it.

Doing a countdown is a good way to keep an eye on your negative thoughts and be ready for them. It's impossible to completely silence your thoughts, but you may reduce their volume to a manageable level.

• Engage in physical activity

The current uptick in the popularity of mind–body exercise programs for groups is more evidence that physical activity is effective for mood improvement. As such, it ranks as one of the most crucial strategies for banishing destructive ideas.

Intelligent fitness buffs have been doing this for years by enrolling in IntenSati, a groundbreaking mind-body exercise that involves training the mind to say happy ideas and employ the intents from class in daily life. The phrase "All negative thoughts cease right now!" is often said aloud by students in the classroom.

Exercising might be a dreary task, but with the help of programs like IntenSati, it can become something that is both rewarding and beneficial to your well-being.

This kind of exercise is so effective that it may even boost brain and social power.

As an added bonus, it may help you feel better about yourself and over time help you understand the significance of choosing to live a life that you like.

• Alter your surroundings

It's not simple to train one's mind to stop dwelling on unpleasant things. But a change in environment, as simple as leaving the area you're in, might inspire fresh ideas.

Raise yourself to your feet and exit the scene. Shift your attention to something else, possibly fresh and improved outlook on folding clothes.

If you're chilling in your room and worrying thoughts start to creep in, you may want to open a window and get some fresh air. One may go the additional mile by strolling about one's neighbourhood. You'll be able to access fresh resources as a result, allowing you to transfer your attention to something else.

If you follow this advice, you could even start to like folding clothes.

• Document it

Avoid dwelling on anything negative; it will only sap your spirit. You should give yourself five to ten minutes to jot down your concerns. When you're through, just toss that list in the trash after you've crumpled it up and ripped it into pieces. Do some venting and then move on.

Writing helps us think more rationally and clearly, and it also serves as an outlet for stress. It's an opportunity to reframe your perspective and take back some control over your life. When you're having trouble getting started, this will be a huge assistance.

• Make use of affirmations

Are you interested in finding out how to put an end to destructive mental processes? Get ready to offer something encouraging to yourself when you have a bad idea. To give you an example, "Sure, I can. I can do it. I am in the process of finding it out." Look for one that resonates with you and keep it around to counteract your inner critic.

It need not be a whole sentence. It's possible that all it takes to convey your intended message to oneself is a simple word or phrase. Say it to yourself over and again until the bad ideas stop bothering you.

If you want to start the day in a good and light mood without allowing any negative ideas in, try saying some affirmations.

• Rely on a stock phrase

Have a good time with this. If you find yourself having negative thinking, try responding to it with something lighthearted or humorous. Stick out your tongue, smack your hand, or flash a grin. Identify a physical reaction that will help you stop thinking and return your attention to the here and now. You may learn to avoid more downward spirals by following this advice.

When you link your attempt to suppress bad ideas with a specific behaviour, you may shift your attention from the thought itself to the response it elicits. The accompanying notion merely recedes into the background as the unfavourable emotion dissipates.

You won't go far without consistently using this method. The effort spent honing your skills will be well worth it.

• Do not pass judgment

When we let ourselves be sucked into a black hole of negative thinking, we are typically our own worst critics. "How stupid of me to not see this coming." The thought that this was feasible shocked me. Someone may be asking, "What is wrong with me? I always seem to screw up the same way. When will I ever learn?"

You should attempt taking the position of an objective observer the next time you find yourself in the midst of a negative thinking pattern. Try to detach yourself from your thoughts and look on. When we're emotionally invested in something, it might be difficult to step back and see how absurd our own thinking has become.

Taking on the role of an observer is like holding up a mirror to our own minds. Being able to look at our own thinking without passing judgment is crucial. As we gain distance from the situation, we are better able to perceive and understand details that previously eluded us.

- **Stop judging yourself based on how others act**

To understand how to rid of destructive beliefs, this is a crucial piece of advice. Today's online community makes it simple to evaluate oneself in relation to others. Scientists found that Facebook users who log in for longer periods of time had more symptoms of depression.

Status updates and images posted online are often used to brag about one's accomplishments, and users often choose to portray themselves in a positive light. It's easy to feel inadequate when compared to the perfect lives your friends portray on Facebook. Then you decide to submit an update that positively portrays you, but you don't receive many reactions to it, leading you to believe that your Facebook friends don't like you.

A lot of this also applies to those who are in committed partnerships. They often follow suit since they've seen their peers doing so. Seeing someone else's happy status in the fake world of social media can be a huge downer if your own romantic life isn't fulfilling. Unconsciously, you begin to evaluate yourself in relation to others.

CHAPTER ———— 14

How To Live A Full Life

M ost of us have to balance professional and personal commitments, and it's not simple to figure out how to do so. Why?

For some of us, the length of our lives is less important than the fact that we lived them to their fullest potential, with joy and no regrets. But how many of us get to go through life to the fullest extent possible? There are moments when it sounds more like a dream than a realistic possibility.

It's possible that the pressure of regular life has gotten to you. Perhaps you just don't think you have the vigour or stamina to get things done. It's also possible that you've never really realised your own potential and talents, and as a result, you've never tried to strike a good balance between them.

Some people may argue that you need to be filthy wealthy to avoid worrying about things like having a job, making ends meet, and feeding your family. Though it's true that having plenty of money may help, I'm relieved to report that it's not necessary.

Here's the reality though:

> We can't keep sacrificing one aspect of ourselves to advance in another. True happiness is impossible for anybody under these circumstances.

In truth, several facets of your existence are interconnected and dependent on one another. Poor health may affect all aspects of your life, from your personal relationships to your professional achievements.

Trading off one item to get another right now may seem like a good idea at the time, but it will have serious long-term repercussions that you cannot see coming. These repercussions will likely be difficult to undo.

The trick is to thrive at whatever you do, not only strike a balance between different aspects of life.

When Have You Lived a Complete Life?

There are six facets of life that require attention if you want to maximise your potential. It would be a mistake to ignore any of them.

There are two main ideas that are crucial to living a fulfilled life: life aspects and core skills.

These ideas originated in my early professional years when I had already exhausted myself via excessive effort.

Being sick sapped my willpower, and I couldn't get the will to continue working. Because of this, I lost faith in myself and my ability to think beyond the box.

However, it wasn't all awful. I exploited the downtime to get some things done. I learned the hard way that excess of any kind is unsustainable and that a balanced approach to life is necessary for attaining happiness, health, and success.

Thus, the six pillars of life aspects were established, each of which must be in harmony for us to operate at our best.

Now let's examine the six facets of living.

1. Good condition of the body

Think of all you could do if you were always fuelled by a boundless supply of motivation and vitality. You can do a lot for your physical and emotional well-being by making some simple changes, such as eating better, getting more exercise, and practicing meditation. You should expect to see improvements across the board as a result of this.

2. The happiness of one's family and other relationships

Maintaining healthy connections is essential to our happiness and success in life. If you can, spend more time with positive, encouraging, and creative individuals and less time with those who are negative.

3. Success in your career and in your job

By setting your sights on professional advancement, you'll have something to work for. The pursuit of one's own happiness has been demonstrated to increase that happiness.

4. Material possessions

Money is not the source of all evil, despite common belief to the contrary. It's all about the cash. Your main objective should be to provide some kind of valuable service to people all around the world. If it's something people really want, you should be able to set a reasonable price for it and reap the financial benefits of that system.

5. Religious and moral health

Though I consider myself primarily a rational person, I do not think every choice and move must be based on facts and statistics. It's important to trust one's gut and emotions every once in a while. Spiritual activities such as meditation, deep breathing, and singing may open you up to a realm beyond reason, regardless of whether or not you believe in a higher force.

6. The capacity of the mind

If someone has a feeble intellect, it will be obvious to everyone. They are undisciplined and aimless and without conviction and willpower. On the other hand, it's not hard to detect someone who has a sharp intellect. Their energy, focus, and interest will be infectious. You'll get the impression that they're a "get-it-done" kind of person.

I suggest you give some serious thought to the six life aspects. Evaluate the situation to determine where restrictions are warranted and where new opportunities might be explored.

When you've achieved harmony between the six life aspects, you can really say that you're working smarter.

The Secret of Happiness

You may be wondering what steps you may take to achieve a healthy equilibrium in each of the six life aspects.

The desire to study is the first step in pursuing a meaningful life.

How long has it been since you last set foot in a classroom? If you're a fully grown, employed adult, odds are it's been quite some time. What about those occasions when you had to get up for morning classes? Remember those times you had to speed through an assignment? Of course, there were also the many tests for which you had to prepare.

Learning is a way of life for lifelong learners; it is something they do on their own will. In addition to expanding one's horizons and enriching one's career prospects, lifelong learning also has the potential to raise one's overall standard of living.

One of the greatest benefits of lifelong learning is the increased flexibility it affords. In today's fast-paced job environment, it is becoming typical for midlife workers to successfully switch careers and spend some time learning on the job.

A new beginning is always possible, regardless of how old you may be. When you invest in your own learning and open yourself up to other perspectives, you expand your horizons and your options. If you aren't happy or content in your present situation, this will provide you with a path out.

Temporary and part-time employment with more adaptable schedules is becoming the norm in today's market. We need to adjust to the new realities of the workplace, improve ourselves by

leaving our comfort zones, and shatter preconceived notions about our capabilities and the direction of our lives.

The Paradigm for a Complete Life

The Full Life Framework consists of five basic tenets that, when followed, may lead to an abundant and satisfying existence.

1. Purposes in life

You give your life meaning with the pursuit of your life's missions. When you accomplish these goals, you will feel a sense of fulfilment, satisfaction, and significance in your life.

Becoming a children's novelist, for example, may be considered a life purpose. Alternatively, the task at hand may focus on the dynamics inside your own family. You may make a change in every area of your life, including health.

Whether or not you are aware of it, you have a purpose in life. They are hardwired into your mind and explain why you care so much about certain issues.

But knowing what they are is a prerequisite for exercising effective command. What motivates you, what makes you get out of bed in the morning, is something you need to be aware of on a conscious level.

2. It's better to make concessions in approach than in goal.

Sacrificing or ignoring your life's true purpose is a painful and miserable experience. A debt is incurred as a result. Furthermore, the longer you put off dealing with it, the more invested you get in the issue.

Ninety-nine percent of teams compromise their goals. They give up what matters most because they think it will make a difference in the long run.

Example: putting aside personal ambitions because you think that's what it takes to be a good parent

For example, putting off personal development in favour of professional advancement might cost you dearly in terms of your relationships.

You know what though? There is never a good reason to do this. To make such a sacrifice is to invite nothing but sorrow.

The issue is that most individuals think they are helpless and have no options. In fact, they do. There is an option open to you. That's why we hold firm to the principle of "bending the rules, not the goals."

Every problem has a solution. Rather than giving up, try modifying your approach. However, to be in a position to make that decision, you'll need to acquire the necessary knowledge and develop the appropriate attitude.

3. The attitude of progress

You must first free yourself from the need to win or lose. Humans are paralysed by a fear of failure, which prevents them from ever embracing the chance for personal development that comes with taking risks.

Success and failure are meaningless to those with a growth attitude. As long as development is being made, that is all that matters to them. If you can bring about development and enhancement, then you have succeeded.

Achieving success requires the introduction of change and development. As long as you continue to improve with each attempt, you will ultimately prevail.

Just picture yourself using this line of reasoning in many contexts.

4. Consistency

Having a "growth attitude" isn't sufficient on its own. Not even in your mind will do! You need the ability to behave in a consistent manner.

Consistency refers to behaviour that is stable and reliable across time.

However, it takes a lot of strength of character and effort to do it. And if there's one thing that study and practice over the last decade have taught us, it's that willpower alone isn't enough to get you through in the long run.

You ought to be able to do the task with little difficulty. You need to have that "autopilot" ability.

This is where autonomous decision-making systems come in handy. Systems like this let you automate your typical ways of thinking and acting. Then taking steps towards your goals in life will become as natural as sitting back and enjoying a good show on TV.

You may be wondering, "What separates high achievers from the rest of the pack?" That's what it is. Those who consistently perform at a high level find ways to incorporate their success into their daily routines.

And so . . .

"Turning daily struggles into opportunities"

CPSIA information can be obtained
at www.ICGtesting.com
Printed in the USA
LVHW032118280323
742863LV00017B/247